PSYCHOLOGICAL TYPES
AND
THE SEVEN RAYS

by
Kurt Abraham

LAMPUS PRESS
19611 Antioch Road
White City, Oregon 97503

Dedicated to
Mary Bailey

Books by Kurt Abraham

Introduction to the Seven Rays

Psychological Types and the Seven Rays

Threefold Method for Understanding the Seven Rays and Other
Essays in Esoteric Psychology

The Seven Rays and Nations: France and the United States
Compared

The Moon Veils Vulcan and the Sun Veils Neptune

Balancing the Pairs of Opposites; The Seven Rays and
Education; and Other Essays in Esoteric Psychology

Orders direct to publisher are welcomed. For current price list
and ordering information, write to:

Lampus Press
19611 Antioch Road
White City, OR 97503

CREDITS

For permission to use copyright material the author gratefully acknowledges the following:

Lucis Trust for permission to quote from Alice A. Bailey's *Esoteric Psychology*, vol. I and II, and *Discipleship in the New Age*, vol. I. The material from Alice Bailey's books may not be reprinted without permission from the Lucis Trust which holds copyright.

Macmillan Publishing Co. for permission to quote from Jane Addams' *Twenty Years at Hull House*, copyright 1910 by Macmillan Publishing Co., Inc., renewed 1983 by James W. Linn.

Little, Brown and Company for permission to quote from *The Complete Letters of Vincent Van Gogh*, New York Graphic Society, 1958. All rights reserved.

Public Affairs Press for permission to quote from Gandhi's *Autobiography*.

Contents

Chapter I

Introduction to the Seven Rays and the Three Types of Mind

The Seven Rays. The very abstruse subject matter of the seven rays was presented to the public in *The Secret Doctrine, the Synthesis of Science, Religion and Philosophy* by H. P. Blavatsky (1888) and was later elaborated in a five volume series of books called *A Treatise on the Seven Rays* by Alice A. Bailey.[1] The seven rays have been defined as "the seven breaths of the one Life, the seven basic energies." "Through the seven rays, the life or spirit aspect flows, cycling through every kingdom in nature and producing thus all states of consciousness in all fields of awareness." "In fact there is nothing in the whole solar system, at whatever stage of evolution it may stand, which does not belong and has not always belonged to one or other of the seven rays." "A ray is but a name for a particular force or type of energy, with the emphasis upon the quality which that force exhibits and not upon the form aspect which it creates. This is a true definition of a ray."[2]

If the seven rays "produce all states of consciousness" and if a ray is a "particular force or type of energy", is there any way in which we can "see" the rays, verify the existence of the rays and make use of the knowledge of the rays in an immediate and practical manner? One of the areas in which the rays can be detected—and also perhaps the first and easiest area—is that of psychology or the scientific study of the consciousness aspect of a human being. In other words, the rays can be detected working out in our own lives; and, as we are able to differentiate the various qualified energies working through us, we become increasingly capable of identifying the qualified energies of a similar nature working through the lives of others, both individually and collectively.

The seven rays or the "seven breaths of the one Life" have been characterized with the following qualifying terms:

1

Ray One: The Ray of Power or Will.

Ray Two: The Ray of Love Wisdom.

Ray Three: The Ray of Intelligent Activity.

Ray Four: The Ray of Harmony Through Conflict.

Ray Five: The Ray of Concrete Knowledge and Science.

Ray Six: The Ray of Devotion and Idealism.

Ray Seven: The Ray of Organization, Ceremonial Order or Magic

We are given several clues as to how it is possible to determine the ray energy in the life of a human being. We are told, for instance, that rays one, four and five "govern with increasing power man's mental life and determine his mental body." Rays two and six "govern potently his emotional life and determine the type of his astral [emotional] body." Rays three and seven "govern the vital physical life and the physical body"[3] This is again mentioned in the second volume of *Esoteric Psychology*, to which it is added: "It is by an understanding of these dominant types of force as they condition the various vehicles that the true nature of the problem of psychology will emerge and the right clue to the solution will appear. The above tabulation and statement is one of the most important ever made in this Treatise in connection with psychology."[4] It is also mentioned that the tabulation is "an infallible rule" except in the case of very highly developed or advanced people[5] *

The rays govern an individual through the physical, emotional and mental aspects of the personality, through the personality itself and through the soul or higher Self. Thus there are *five rays* that can directly affect and govern an individual. Indirectly, or as a group effect, there are a great many other ray influences playing upon and governing various aspects of a person's life. The soul or higher Self can be on any one of the seven rays.[6] The personality also can be on any one of the seven rays. And, as mentioned, the rays of the three aspects of the personality fall into the following pattern:

Mind ....ray 1, 4 or 5

Emotional body.................................. ray 2 or 6

Physical body..................................... ray 3 or 7

In way of brief definition: the *emotional body* deals with the sentient, feeling nature. It is visible to clairvoyant sight and

---

*See appendix for clarification of exceptions to rule.

is "composed of matter of an order of fineness higher than that of physical matter, in which feelings, passions, desires and emotions are expressed and which acts as a bridge or medium of transmission between the physical brain and the mind"[7] "Through the sensory vehicle the astral or emotional nature originates the bulk of those desires and impulses which direct the undeveloped or average man, and which can be called desire-impulses or the wish-life of the individual."[8]

The *mental body* is composed of yet a subtler and finer substance and is also visible to highly developed clairvoyant sight. Whereas the emotional-feeling nature knows vaguely through a sensitivity of similarity, through a state of being en rapport with something else, the mental nature knows through analysis, reason and detached observation. Whereas the astral-emotional body is sensitive to feeling states and moods, the mental body becomes intellectually sensitive and responsive to nuances of ideas and thoughts.

The *personality* is a distinctive state of consciousness that emerges as the physical, emotional and mental natures are developed, coordinated and integrated. The colloquial expression of being a "together" person designates somewhat this developed and integrated state. Power to influence the environment for good or ill increases, as does a sense of personal identity, self-will and self-determination. The ray of the personality only emerges in outer, demonstrated clarity and influence when this state of coordination of the developed mind and developed emotions occurs.[9] Abraham Maslow's definition of a "self-actualized" person is very similar to the definition of personality as it is used here. The integrated personality has a great deal more to say about the determination of his own destiny than does the non-integrated person, who is buffeted about by circumstances and who acquiescently hopes for the best.

The *soul* or *higher Self* deals with yet a subtler, more refined level of consciousness than that of the personality, intellect and emotional natures. The soul also has a form nature, which is known as the "causal body" in Theosophical literature, and this unit too is visible to highly developed clairvoyant sight.[10] Of the higher Self Roberto Assagioli states: "This Self is above, and unaffected by, the flow of the mind-stream or by bodily conditions; and the personal conscious self should be considered merely as its reflection, its 'projection' in the field of the personality. At the present stage of psychological investigation little is definitely known concerning the Self, but the importance of this synthesizing center well warrants further research."[11] He also states that the "real distinguishing factor between the little self [personality] and the higher Self is that the little self is acutely aware of itself as a distinct separate individual, and a sense of solitude or of separation sometimes comes in the existential experience. In contrast, the experience of the spiritual Self is a sense of freedom, of expansion, of communication with other Selves and with reality, and there is the sense of Universality. It feels itself at the same time individual and universal."[12] As the personality begins to integrate with the soul and as the life and consciousness of the soul begin to manifest through and dominate the life of the personality, then the ray of the soul becomes more "visible," more observable in the activity of the outer life.

Purpose for Studying Psychological Types. There are primarily three purposes for studying psychological types. First of all, we study psychological types in order to *"know thyself."* Each type has qualities, characteristics and tendencies peculiar to itself. A study of types enables one to gain conscious recognition of those characteristics and tendencies, thereby gaining knowledge of the individual unit. The individual part or type, however, becomes conscious of itself in relation to other parts or types. Initially there is the tendency to gravitate toward similarity of type and to exclude dissimilar types. Eventually, however, a gradual appreciation grows for the collective life and consciousness that is working out or manifesting through diversified outer parts or types. This leads us to the second purpose: *we study types in order to see the whole to which the type is but a part.* With the recognition of the whole we are then on our way towards *being the whole* in a relative sense.

The confinement to type is only a temporary limitation. Confinement to type enables one to develop in a specialized, concentrated, focussed fashion. Over-specialization, however, can lead to an imbalance that threatens the good of the whole, whether that whole is the psychological development of a human being, a community, a nation or a planet. Ignorance has been defined as "mistaking the part for the whole." Ignorance, therefore, is not so much a state of not knowing as it is a state of being knowledgeable about a part and refusing to accept the greater responsibility, labor and sacrifice of becoming knowledgeable about the interrelated and complementary parts that constitute the whole. Ignorance is related to inertia and to the following of a path of least resistance. In other words, once we have gone through the labor of acquring skill and knowledge in a particular area of endeavor, there is a tendency to continue to negate and minimize the value of areas of endeavor that are totally foreign to us. This temporarily frees one from the additional labor and responsibility of becoming the whole, but it leads to the sad anomoly of the imbalanced specialist fighting to perpetuate a field of study, a discipline, an institution, a business, etc., that is becoming a threat to the well-being of the whole. The part either makes a valuable contribution to the whole, or the part, engrossed in the illusions generated by self-interest, endeavors to usurp the whole. Interestingly, the labor to correct our failures due to mistaking the part for the whole seems in many cases to be greater and certainly more painful than the labor along those paths of sacrifice and new beginnings that lead to the whole.

In the working out of parts and wholes, for the whole of one system is but a particular part of another, certain patterns emerge. This leads us to our third purpose for studying types. Through our knowledge of what the parts are and how they interelate within a whole system, we can then proceed more intelligently, less harmfully, less painfully and more clearly in the relatively larger whole to which the previous whole is but a part. This we can do because of the *law of analogy*.

> One of the main means whereby man arrives at an understanding of that great sum total we call the Macrocosm—God, functioning through a solar system—is by an understanding of himself, and the Delphic injunction "man, know thyself" was an inspired utterance, intended to give man the clue to the mystery of deity. Through the Law of Analogy, or correspondences, the cosmic processes, and the nature of the cosmic principles are indicated in the functions, structures, and characteristics of a human being. They are indicated but not explained or elaborated. They serve simply as sign posts, directing man along the path whereon future sign posts may be found and more definite indications noted.[13]

In a certain sense we can think of the psychological aspect of a human being known as the personality as beginning and developing the work of knowing thyself, the part, the specialized unit. This the soul carries to completion as it enhances the self knowledge of the part in cooperation with the good of the whole. In the soul consciousness love of the whole supersedes the indentification with the separative part. The instinct of self-preservation is replaced by the instinct of selfless service. The soul, the embodiment of unity, begins the further work of being the whole, of developing in a relative sense the qualities and consciousness of all the seven rays.

In our effort to recognize a particular ray energy as it colors the psychological make-up of a human being and predisposes him toward certain tendencies and types of attitudes and activities, it will be necessary to call attention again and again to the underlying theme of wholeness. This is especially necessary, since the focus will be on the three types of mind—on a part.

A little study of the seven rays and months or years of observation will bring the careful observer to the realization that this is not an arbitrary typology; it is not a speculative system that we seek to impose on nature. It deals, on the contrary, with the fact of conditioning, qualified energies that are visible to most of us not in their pure form but in their effects. The matter, however, is difficult in that the interweaving of the seven rays condition and permeate all aspects of life and affect a human being on so many levels that it becomes a matter of immense complexity. On the other hand, the seven rays in themselves provide us with a synthesizing simplicity that enables one step by step to discern the majestic order running through the apparently unfathomable complexity.

Before getting into the three types of mind themselves, it is necessary to recognize that there is a sequential unfoldment of the various units of sentiency and consciousness and therefore of the rays governing the various units. For example, there are a great many people who have not as yet developed the intellect or lower mind to any appreciable degree and therefore the ray of the mind can hardly be detected. At this early stage "the rays governing the physical and emotional bodies are dominant. The soul ray is scarcely felt and only flickers with a dim light at the heart of each lotus" or chakra. As the intellect or mental body develops, it develops along a particular line of endeavor, a path of least resistance, conditioned by the mental ray. At this stage of "intellection" much can be said about how the three rays that condition the mind dispose one to various characteristics and tendencies and reveal certain assets, talents and refinement as well as certain prejudices and limitations. As the mind develops, the "coordination" of the three aspects of the personality—the physical, emotional and mental units—also steadily takes place and the ray of the personality begins to emerge with greater clarity. During the following stages "the soul ray comes into increased conflict with the personality ray and the great battle of the pairs of opposites begins. The soul ray or energy slowly dominates the personality ray, as it in its turn has dominated the rays of the three lower bodies"[14]

There is a pattern then of (1) a focus on the development of a particular unit or aspect, (2) a transition period of conflict and interplay between a developed unit and the next higher or more refined unit, (3) followed by a period of integration and stabilization when the various units function in a coordinated fashion and as a relative whole.

The stage of "intellection" is of particular interest in that it provides a period wherein the ray of the mental unit can be clearly differentiated, revealing psychological factors of considerable moment.

The First Ray Type. The seven rays can be related to each other in the following manner:

> Rays 1. 3. 7 are the great rays connected with the form, with the evolutionary process, with the intelligent functioning of the system, and with the laws controlling the life in all forms in all the kingdoms in nature.
>
> Rays 2. 4. 6 are the rays connected with the inner life, expanding through those forms,—the rays of motive, aspiration and sacrifice. Rays pre-eminently of quality.
>
> Rays 1. 3. 7 deal with things concrete and with the functioning of matter and form from the lowest plane to the highest.
>
> Rays 2. 4. 6 deal with things abstract, with spiritual expression through the medium of form.
>
> Ray 5 ... forms the connecting link of the intelligence.[15]

The first ray is the ray of will, purpose and power. The first ray type has been called "the power type, full of will and governing capacity."[16] As the first ray conditions the mental body, one finds the "governing capacity" being translated into administrative and managerial skills. Administrative work deals "with the form ... with the intelligent functioning of the sytem ... and with things concrete."

Certain positive qualities tend to emerge with the first ray type, such as a sense of responsibility, strength, determination, endurance, recognition of power and the power structure, impersonality, detachment, leadership, willfulness, emotional control, organizational and administrative capacities. Negatively, these characteristics can become selfish ambition, hardness, aggressiveness, cruelty, arrogance, a pre-occupation with personal power, materialism, the controlling and manipulating of others. When there is a lack of the balancing sensitivity and love of the two-four-six line, the concern "with things concrete and with the functioning of matter and form" can become hard, unyielding, cold and domineering.

The first ray mind has also been called the "map-making and plan-formulating mind." The plan-formulating mind is concerned with detailed programs of practical action.

Fourth Ray Type. The fourth ray is one of the three rays connected with the inner life and with things abstract. The fourth ray type has been called the "artistic type, full of the sense of beauty and creative aspiration." Although artists can be found on all the rays, when "the mental vehicle is governed by an elemental of fourth ray nature or quality, ... creative, artistic activity is the line of least resistance."[17] This does not mean, however, that every person with a fourth ray mind becomes an artist. But there is an "artistic" mode of thinking that may tend to find creative expression in one of the arts.

Certain positive qualities tend to emerge with the fourth ray type, such as a sense of creativity, of imagination, of beauty and color, an ability to conciliate, to harmonize and to find a balanced middle path. There may also be sympathy, compassion, serenity and an ability to align with the intuition. On the negative side one may find a tendency to fluctuate between extremes, a fighting for the sake of conflict, impatience, impracticality, emotionalism, and difficulty with organization.

This has been called the "ray of struggle" for on this ray the qualities of rajas (activity) and tamas (inertia) are so strangely equal in proportion that the nature of the fourth ray man is torn with their combat, and the outcome, when satisfactory, is spoken of as the "Birth of Horus," of the Christ, born from the throes of constant pain and suffering.

Tamas induces love of ease and pleasure, a hatred of causing pain amounting to moral cowardice, indolence, procrastination, a desire to let things be, to rest, and to take no thought of the morrow. Rajas is fiery, impatient, ever urging to action. These contrasting forces in nature make life one perpetual warfare and unrest for the fourth ray man; the friction and the experience gained thereby may produce very rapid evolution, but the man may as easily become a ne'er-do-well as a hero.[18]

Fifth Ray Type. The fifth ray forms "the connecting link of intelligence" between the concrete and the abstract worlds. The fifth ray type has been called the "scientific type, full of the ideas of cause and results."[19] The main characteristic of the fifth ray type of mind is clarity of thought and precise knowledge. Exactitude of knowledge, expertise, can only be gained in a limited area, so there is the necessity for specialization. Intellect and reason receive a greater emphasis than the imagination, feeling, and intuition of the fourth ray type. Also pure knowledge or pure research is generally of greater interest than the practical action and the administrative overview of the first ray type.

Some of the positive characteristics that emerge with fifth ray types are clarity of thought, careful reasoning, precise and accurate observation, detachment, love of knowledge, effort to determine cause, analysis, caution, and power to master a chosen field of knowledge. Some negative characteristics that may emerge are narrow specialization, skepticism to the point of prejudice, lack of a creative imagination, mental crystallization, criticism and pride.

REFERENCE NOTES TO CHAPTER I

1. The five volumes of Alice Bailey's *A Treatise on the Seven Rays* (New York: Lucis Publishing Co.) are: *Esoteric Psychology*, I (1936), *Esoteric Psychology*, II (1942), *Esoteric Astrology* (1951), *Esoteric Healing* (1953). and *The Rays and the Initiations* (1960).
2. Bailey, *Esoteric Psychology*, I, pp. 44, 60, 163, 316.
3. Ibid., pp. 320-1.
4. Bailey, *Esoteric Psychology*, II, p. 288.
5. Alice Bailey, *Glamour: A World Problem* (New York: Lucis Publishing Co., 1950), p. 92.
6. Bailey, *Esoteric Psychology*, I, pp. 321, 401.
7. Arthur E. Powell, *The Astral Body* (London: The Theosophical Publishing House, 1927), p. 1.
8. Bailey, *Esoteric Psychology*, II, p. 406.
9. Ibid., p. 334.
10. See Arthur E. Powell's *The Causal Body and the Ego* (London: The Theosophical Publishing House, 1928), and Charles W. Leadbeater's *Man Visible and Invisible* (Adyar, India: The Theosophical Publishing House, 1925; rpt. as Quest Book, 1972).
11. Roberto Assagioli, *Psychosynthesis* (1965; rpt. New York: Penguin Books, 1976), p. 19.
12. Ibid., p. 87.
13. Alice Bailey, *A Treatise on White Magic* (New York: Lucis Publishing Co., 1934), p. 18.
14. Bailey, *Esoteric Psychology*, II, pp. 306-9.
15. Bailey, *Esoteric Psychology*, I, p. 89.
16. Ibid., p. 329.
17. Bailey, *Esoteric Psychology*, II, p. 292.
18. Bailey, *Esoteric Psychology*, I, p. 207.
19. Ibid., p. 329.

Chapter II
Jane Addams:
First Ray Mind

Jane Addams (Cedarville, Illinois, 1860-1935) became known as a social worker and humanitarian. She founded the Hull-House in Chicago, a "Settlement" or community service center, from which she carried on a great variety of innovative, philanthropic, social service activities. Her book *Twenty Years at Hull-House with Autobiographical Notes* gives us some insight into her life and her thinking processes.

Initial Attempt at a Scientific Career. When Jane Addams was a college student, the work of such people as Darwin and Thomas Huxley was beginning to sweep through the academic community. The new science was having its effect.

> In the long vacations I pressed plants, stuffed birds and pounded rocks in some vague belief that I was approximating the new method, and yet when my step-brother who was becoming a real scientist, tried to carry me along with him into the merest outskirts of the method of research, it at once became evident that I had no aptitude and was unable to follow intelligently Darwin's careful observations of the earthworm. I made an heroic effort, although candor compels me to state that I never would have finished if I had not been pulled and pushed by my really ardent companion, who in addition to a multitude of earthworms and a fine microscope, possessed untiring tact with one of flagging zeal.[1]

There is a tendency among many who have first ray minds to have an interest in science but to lack the "zeal" or the perseverance that would enable them to carve out a career in a scientific field. It remains at the hobby level. This is most certainly, however, not always the case! A fifth or seventh ray influence at the personality or soul level could bring about the needed capacity for a refined and sustained effort in a scientific field.

11

After graduating from college with a liberal arts background, she attended the Woman's Medical College of Philadelphia with the intent of becoming a physician. Her propelling interest, however, was not science, not medicine, but helping the poor. She was an idealistic young person who, inspired by the lives of great humanitarians, was aspiring to a life of service. She was acutely conscious of the glaring needs of the time brought on by the infant industrial society. In choosing to study medicine, she was gravitating towards the first and most obvious form of service that presented itself. The study of medicine was a means to some other end (social action) rather than an end in itself (knowledge).

During the first winter of her medical studies Jane Addams was forced to withdraw due to a spinal difficulty that had bothered her since childhood.

> In spite of its tedium, the long winter had its mitigations, for after the first weeks I was able to read with a luxurious consciousness of leisure, and I remember opening the first volume of Carlyle's *Frederick the Great* with a lively sense of gratitude that it was not Gray's *Anatomy*, having found, like many another that general culture is a much easier undertaking than professional study. [She passed her examinations in the required subject for the first year but] was very glad to have a physician's sanction for giving up clinics and dissecting rooms and to follow his prescriptions of spending the next two years in Europe.
>
> Before I returned to America I had discovered that there were other genuine reasons for living among the poor than that of practicing medicine among them, and my brief foray into the profession was never resumed.[2]

Her difficulty with medical study was not due to a lack of intelligence, but rather to the *type* of intelligence "conditioned" by the fifth ray of scientific knowledge.

Struggle to Formulate a Plan of Action. Realizing that medicine was not the right path for her, there remained yet the long struggle to determine the direction her life should take ("should" in the sense of aligning the inner sensed purpose with outer actualization).

Whatever may have been the perils of self-tradition, I certainly did not escape them, for it required eight years—from the time I left Rockford in the summer of 1881 until Hull-House was opened in the autumn of 1889—to formulate my convictions even in the least satisfactory manner, much less to reduce them to a plan for action. During most of that time I was absolutely at sea so far as any moral purpose was concerned, clinging only to the desire to live in a really living world and refusing to be content with a shadowy intellectual or aesthetic reflection of it.[3]

During this time of being "absolutely at sea" and struggling to differentiate between what was truly coming from the depths of her nature and what was imposed on her through tradition and education, she was travelling around Europe with a small group of college friends. One of their primary activities was to absorb the culturally rich experience that Europe had to offer. They attended concerts, went to the theatre, read the literature, went to art galleries, etc. She was beginning to reject, however, that which she called the "aesthetic reflection" of the "really living world." Intellectual and aesthetic abstractions were being negated in favor of things concrete. From her point of view there was a hiatus between the aesthetic experience and the necessities of physical plane living.

The "really living world" revealed to her another picture as she observed the poverty of East London. Every Saturday night decaying vegetables and fruits were auctioned off to the poor. Upon securing a piece of produce, the successful bidder "instantly sat down on the curb, tore it with his teeth, and hastily devoured it, unwashed and uncooked as it was ... Their pale faces were dominated by that most unlovely of human expressions, the cunning and shrewdness of the bargain hunter who starves if he cannot make a successful trade ... For the following weeks I went about London almost furtively, afraid to look down narrow streets and alleys lest they disclose again this hideous human need and suffering."[4]

Jane Addams, with some pain, had eliminated the possibility of pursuing a career in science. Now she was repulsing the world of culture and the arts, the aesthetic sense associated with the fourth ray. This was not easy, for in many ways (education and friends) it constituted the predominate influence in her environment.

"Lumbering Our Minds with Literature." She recalled De Quincey's "The Vision of Sudden Death" in which he finds himself in a momentary paralysis during an emergency situation. Instead of calling out to two absorbed lovers in order to warn them of the threat of an approaching mail-coach, he finds himself trying to recall the exact lines of a warning cry Achilles uttered in the *Iliad*. Jane Addams reflected:

> This is what we were all doing, lumbering our minds with literature that only served to cloud the really vital situation spread before our eyes. It seemed to me too preposterous that in my first view of the horror of East London I should have recalled De Quincey's literary description of the suggestion which had once paralyzed him. In my disgust it all appeared a hatefully, vicious circle which even the apostles of culture themselves admitted, for had not one of the greatest among the moderns plainly said that "conduct, and not culture is three fourths of human life."[5]

"Conduct", "the really vital situation spread before our eyes", what we do on the physical plane, was becoming more important than intellectual-aesthetic appreciation. There is great practicality in illuminating the mind and in refining the emotional sensitivities through cultural works. Improving the mind and sentient nature is foundational to improving the physical realities. But it was apparently necessary to reject one mode of endeavor in order to concentrate on another. Medicine was discovered to be too difficult; cultural edification was discovered to be an impediment to dealing with the "really living world"—judgements due largely, it seems to me, to the natural affinities and antipathies resulting from ray type.

"Pictures as Human Documents." During her two month stay in Dresden, Jane Addams and her friends spent much time reading art history and visiting the art galleries and opera house. She noted that:

> [A]fter such an experience I would invariably suffer a moral revulsion against this feverish search for culture. It was doubtless in such moods that I founded my admiration for Albrecht Durer, taking his wonderful pictures, however, in the most unorthodox manner, merely as human documents. I was chiefly appealed to by his unwillingness to lend himself to a smooth and cultivated view

of life, by his determination to record its frustrations and even the hideous forms which darken the day for our human imagination and to ignore no human complications.[6]

Apparently, the dominant note of the group was—as she negatively described it—that of a "feverish search for culture" against which she had a "moral revulsion." Her own preference in art was for Dürer's "human documents"—the more physically accurate representations that did not ignore the hideous forms nor any "human complications." This is in contrast to the sort of painting that presents a "smooth and cultivated view of life", which suggest a more idyllic representation and a greater concern for beauty and harmony and for the ideal.

It must have been no simple task for her to find her own direction in life, surrounded as she was by those who—at the level of the intellect—sounded a different note and responded to a different vibration. The group apparently shared a deep concern for the welfare of their brothers and sisters in the human family. The differences were more in method and strategy than in principle. Jane Addams was beginning to formulate plans of practical action to alleviate immediate physical plane needs.

Establishing the Institution—The Beginning of Hull-House. During her travels she visited the Toynbee Hall in East London. Toynbee Hall was the first "Settlement" or philanthropic community center that eventually was to inspire many such centers in England and in the major metropolitan areas of the United States. The Settlements administered to a great many of the acute needs of poor people and were also instrumental in bringing about key social legislation (child labor laws, workman's compensation, sanitary working conditions, etc.).

Jane Addams returned to the United States with the intent to "rent a house in a part of the city where many primitive and actual needs are found." But she was not only thinking of the poor and deprived. She was also concerned that "young women who had been given over too exclusively to study, might restore a balance of activity along traditional lines and learn of life from life itself . . . [and might] try out some of the things they had been taught and put truth to 'the ultimate test of the conduct it dictates or inspires.' "[7] "Our young people feel nervously

15

the need of putting theory into practice and respond quickly to the Settlement form of activity."[8] When the academics are overemphasized, young people in general feel a need to balance the intellectual pursuits with a more grounded activity. The first ray would tend to augment this tendency.

In 1889 she located a house in a depressed area of Chicago that seemed suited to her purposes and leased the second floor. This was known as the Hull-House. At the time of its inception she was twenty-nine years old. She had inherited a sum of money from her father, and this money enabled her to travel and live in Europe. Now she was investing the remainder of the inheritance in Hull-House, for "in those days we made no appeal for money, meaning to start with our own slender resources."[9] Hull-House eventually grew to a complex of thirteen buildings.

"In the very first weeks of our residence Miss Starr started a reading party in George Eliot's *Romola*, which was attended by a group of young women who followed the wonderful tale with unflagging interest." The first activity was a cultural one, and there was a great variety of cultural activities to follow. It is interesting that now there was no complaint that the activity was a "feverish search for culture" or that the romantic tale lacked a living reality, for now it was part of a program of social action which she had instituted. "Volunteers to the new undertakings came quickly; a charming young girl conducted a kindergarten in the drawing-room ... Another memory ... is that of the young girl who organized our first really successful club of boys, holding their fascinated interest by the old chivalric tales, set forth so dramatically and vividly."[10] Reading club, kindergarten, boys' club—eventually the list of activities, groups and organizations became very long. The boys' club grew to a five-story building with "splendid equipment of shops", with recreation facilities and study rooms.

Whereas the fourth ray type of mind tends to be concerned with things abstract, with creative expression, with a psychological or cultural search for beauty and meaning; and the fifth ray scientific type tends to be concerned with accumulating and contributing facts and clear perception to a body of knowledge; the first ray mind tends to be attracted to the "really vital situation spread before our eyes" and tends to want to put "theory into practice" and *to do* something about the concrete situation. This may demonstrate as an effort or an ability to "institutionalize" a program of social service. It may demonstrate as administrative and managerial skills, or as a business acumen, depending partially on other ray influences affecting the individual. Much of the frustration Jane Addams experienced in her twenties dissipated when she involved herself in the work that affected change or dealt with problems at the visibly vital physical level. This suggests that with the first ray type of mind there tends to be a mental-physical alignment or interplay, and there also tends to be a negation or control of the emotional factor. In contrast to this, the fourth ray type of mind tends to aspire to or to achieve an intuitive-emotion alignment and interplay. As a result, there may be a neglectful or vague concern for physical plane detail. The "mind's eye" of the *pronounced* fourth ray type tends to look out over an entirely different world, as we shall see in the lives of van Gogh, Thoreau and Rousseau. In a great many cases, however, the differences of ray type are not so evident as they are in the pronounced types selected here for purposes of clarification.

A Variety of Social Service Activities. Although the activities for children were very successful, Jane Addams did not want to limit Hull-House to children only. "It was absurd to suppose that grown people should not respond to opportunities for education and social life." Also, "from the first it seemed understood that we were ready to perform the humblest neighborhood services. We were asked to wash the new-born babies, and to prepare the dead for burial, to nurse the sick, and to mind the children." [11]

For six weeks after an operation we kept in our three bedrooms a forlorn little baby who, because he was born with a cleft palate, was most unwelcome even to his mother, and we were horrified when he died of neglect a week after he was returned to his home; a little Italian bride of fifteen sought shelter with us one November evening, to escape her husband who had beaten her every night for a week when he returned from work, because she had lost her wedding ring; two of us officiated quite alone at the birth of an illegitimate child because the doctor was late in arriving, and none of the honest Irish matrons would "touch the likes of her"; we ministered at the deathbed of a young man, who during a long illness of tuberculosis had received so many bottles of whiskey through the mistaken kindness of his friends, that the cumulative effect produced wild periods of exultation, in one of which he died.[12]

The above activities deal with emergency situations. Frequently, but certainly not always, one will find the first ray type dealing with the acute situation. The ambulance driver, the policeman or the crisis intervening person is more likely than not to have a first ray mind. What is generally required is some sort of *immediate action* that temporarily alleviates the crisis-precipitating factors. It may be a physical or psychological or technical first-aid treatment. It may be transportation to a treatment center, it may be referral to an agency, it may be restraining a person for a period of time. A high degree of specialized knowledge is generally not required. What is required is a sort of *synthesis* of many different kinds of knowledge. One must be a little bit of the judge, the doctor, the psychologist, the lawyer and the priest, for example, in order to perform the duties of, say, a policeman. We also find that a certain *presence of mind* or *poise* is needed so that one can act in a cool and detached manner. Generally speaking, the fourth ray type with its tendency towards abstraction, sensitivity and identification with the suffering person, tends not to be attracted to emergency work. Also the fifth ray mind with its love of the controlled experimental situation generally tends not to be attracted to this type of work. Some emergency situations, however, can only be met by the specialized expert, such as emergency medical and complex technical situations, and in such cases one may find the first and fifth rays working in some combination.

First Lessons in Power. Jane Addams' concern for the poor quickly brought her in contact with the municipal authorities.

The policy of the public authorities of never taking the initiative, and always waiting to be urged to do their duty, is obviously fatal in a neighborhood where there is little initiative among the citizens. The idea underlying our self-government breaks down in such a ward. The streets are inexpressibly dirty, the number of schools inadequate, sanitary legislation unenforced, the street

18

lighting bad, the paving miserable and altogether lacking in the alleys and smaller streets, and the stables foul beyond description. Hundreds of houses are unconnected with the street sewer. The older and richer inhabitants seem anxious to move away as rapidly as they can afford it. They make room for newly arrived immigrants who are densely ignorant of civic duties.[13]

While others working with her at Hull-House were concerned with cultural and psychological needs, Jane Addams was more specifically concerned with the acute physical needs of the community and with "civic duties." Adequate scientific knowledge already existed to deal with most of the problems cited. Jane Addams quickly realized that she was dealing with factors of power. As a young woman in her late twenties and early thirties, she was beginning to identify the power factor in human interaction with greater clarity and she was learning how to deal with it. Recalling how she balked at the first obstacles put in her way as she tentitively played with a possible career in science, similarly the fourth and fifth ray types would tend to balk at the obstacles along the paths of power. (This tendency, however, could be offset by the first and also the seventh ray conditioning the soul or personality vehicle.) She recognized that the public authorities tend not to take the initiative, tend not "to do their duty" in respect to citizens unless they are urged to do so. And that urging must be from a sufficiently powerful source if the authorities are to respond to it. The strength of the people for whom she worked lay not in their money, not in their position, nor in their intelligence—but solely in their numbers. But as an ununified, scattered force without a spokesperson, they were powerless indeed.

Statistical Studies One of the residents of Hull-House collected facts and information pertaining to the conditions of poverty in the ward and submitted them to the United States Bureau of Labor in conjunction with the Bureau's investigation into "the slums of great cities." These facts along with descriptive writing and reflections on neighborhood conditions were published in a book called *Hull-House Maps and Papers*. Of the three ray types of mind under consideration the first ray type is the one more likely to respond to and generate the documentation and statistical analysis of the human condition. It differs from scientific studies in that the scientific studies look for laws of cause and effect while the statistical studies examine the state of the present condition. While the scientific studies examine those elements that are true for all times (from a relative angle),the factual studies of a first ray nature examine matters that are of the utmost importance today but may be of no consequence tomorrow. Thus, the number of people that live in a particular ward of a city generally has more political significance than scientific interest. Nutrition is a matter of much scientific interest and study. The number of malnourished people living in a district or country is of much political interest, and, thus, documented, statistical evidence of the matter is generally desired. The fourth ray type, generally speaking, tends not to be very good at statistical, fact-finding studies but this type can draw "vivid word-pictures" that appeal to the "heart", the moral, the sensitive factor. We see that the work of Charles Dickens and many such social writers of the day did a great deal in an indirect way to bring about social change.

A Group of Social Activists. A group of service oriented people gathered around Hull-House, joining Jane Addams in her effort to meet the needs of the poor and the suffering through right social action. A residential home was built for the growing number of women working with Hull-House. Soon afterward a men's residential house was opened across the street. They started with the most basic needs and endeavored to take whatever action their limited resources would allow.

One of their earliest projects was a public kitchen. Originally this was instituted in order to make up for the deficiencies in nutrition experienced by factory workers who were too tired to do anything but open a can at the end of the day's labor. Carefully prepared soups and stews were sold in the neighboring factories and to a few families in the neighborhood. Although some frankly confessed that they "did not like to eat what was nutritious" and others were bound to "inherited tastes" along nationality lines, the public kitchen did grow steadily throughout the years.

The public kitchen and coffee house grew to serve other needs and expanded along other lines. At the time the only place in the neighborhood for large social gatherings, such as weddings, dances, special meetings, etc., was the saloon halls. The coffee house (and gymnasium, which was in the same building) gradually came to perform that function as a social center. "Better food was doubtless needed, but more attractive and safer places for social gatherings were also needed, and the neighborhood was ready for one and not the other."[14]

Several of the philanthropic institutions initiated by Hull-House and similar organizations on a small scale were later absorbed by government institutions that were able to meet the needs on a larger scale. "We had no hint then in Chicago of the small parks which were to be established fifteen years later, containing the halls for dancing and their own restaurants in buildings where the natural desire of the young for gayety and social organizations, could be safely indulged."[15] As those parks came into existence, a member of the Hull-House Men's Club was appointed superintendent of Douglas Park, securing there the first public swimming pool.

> I do not wish to give a false impression, for we were often bitterly pressed for money and worried by the prospect of unpaid bills, and we gave up one golden scheme after another because we could not afford it; we cooked the meals and kept the books and washed the windows without a thought of hardship if we thereby saved money for the consummation of some ardently desired undertaking.
>
> But in spite of financial stringency, I always believed that money would be given when we had once clearly reduced the Settlement idea to the actual deed.[16]

After the initial investment of her own limited resources, Hull-House was supported primarily by private contributions and volunteer workers. The ability to deal intelligently, responsibly and creatively with financial matters is a complex and subtle matter that is definitely affected by the rays. Money comes more within the domain of rays one, three and seven than it does within rays two, four and six. Her use of money, one might add, was for the general good, and she asked little, if anything, for her own personal self. This suggests, along with other factors, a considerable degree of personality control and soul alignment.

Christianity Interpreted in Terms of Action and Will. "The Christians looked for the continuous revelation," wrote Jane Addams, "but believed what Jesus said, that this revelation, to be retained and made manifest, must be put into terms of action;

that action is the only medium man has for receiving and appropriating truth; that the doctrine must be known through the will."[17]

It seems to me that there is very clearly here a first ray bias emphasing action and will over all else. To Huxley *fact* could be likened to the Will of God in that: if one wanted to gain knowledge, one ought to sit down before it like a little child. Thoreau held highest in his esteem the poet who "is actuated by pure love." Jane Addams sounded yet a different note, placing action and will at the top of her value system. Similar to Jane Addams, Gandhi saw Christ as a "prince among politicians" and one involved in "intensely direct action." In Jane Addams' words:

> I believe that there is a distinct turning among many young men and women toward this simple acceptance of Christ's message. They resent the assumption that Christianity is a set of ideas which belong to the religious consciousness, whatever that may be. They insist that it cannot be proclaimed and instituted apart from the social life of the community and that it must seek a simple and natural expression in the social organism itself. The Settlement movement is only one manifestation of that wider humanitarian movement which throughout Christendom, but preeminently in England, is endeavoring to embody itself, not in a sect but in society itself.
>
> I believe that this turning, the renaissance of the early Christian humanitarianism, is going on in America, in Chicago, if you please, without leaders who write or philosophize, without much speaking, but with a bent to express in social service and in terms of action the spirit of Christ.[18]

Certainly one cannot take issue with this aspect of the Christ spirit which she emphasized, namely "social service" and "action." Yet again, if this aspect is mistaken for the whole, then vitally important complementary work will either go unrecognized or will be negated. As she earlier rebelled against the "feverish search for culture" and the "lumbering of our minds with literature", now she was being critical of the "religious consciousness, whatever that may be." It is implied that the "religious consciousness" tends more towards writing, philosophizing and speaking than towards social action. Perhaps she was once again trying to come to terms with an ap-.

proach to truth more indicative of the fourth ray type. She emphasized not only social action but a "simple acceptance" and a "simple and natural expression" of Christ's message. In other words complex mental abstractions were being negated in favor of simple, but highly principled, concrete action. The "plan-formulating mind" was turned more towards social action than towards understanding subtle nuances of meaning of a more philosophical or abstract nature.

It seems at this point that the practical action orientation of her first ray mind was being reinforced by another ray along the one-three-five-seven line at either the personality or soul level. The inclusive, self-sacrificing, service tone of her work suggests that the egoic or soul ray was the controlling factor. The organizational emphasis of her work suggests a possible seventh ray influence.

Abstract and Concrete Minds. According to Jane Addams, there was a ten year period when the problems of industrial organization were discussed prior to the social action that led to change. In conclusion she stated:

> . . . I hastily review the decade in Chicago which followed this one given over to discussion, the actual attainment of these early hopes, so far as they have been realized at all, seem to have come from men of affairs rather than from those given to speculation. Was the whole decade of discussion an illustration of that striking fact which has been likened to the changing swords in Hamlet; that the abstract minds at length yield to the inevitable or at least grow less ardent in their propaganda, while the concrete minds, dealing constantly with daily affairs, in the end demonstrate the reality of abstract notions?[19]

The confusion here, it seems to me, is that instead of recognizing how different approaches form vital parts of a whole and that different stages of development require an emphasis on different parts, there was the tendency to reduce the matter into an either/or situation, which brought about a polarization between the different parts. On the one hand, we have the "abstract mind" given over to "discussion", "propaganda" and "speculation", while on the other hand we find "concrete minds" and "men of affairs" demonstrating "actual attainment." The statement "the abstract minds at length yield to the inevitable or at least grow less ardent in their propaganda" definitely colors the matter in a negative way. There is likely a ray-kinship between those "feverishly seeking culture," the "religious consciousness," and now the "abstract minds" who eventually are forced to "grow less ardent in their propaganda." The bottom line, the proof in the pudding, the final word—in Jane Addams' opinion—was not in the abstractions but in the concrete. But a little thought along a holistic framework (such as the rays provide) with personal detachment clearly reveals the complementary necessity of both of these approaches.

In a sense her own work bridged between the abstract and the concrete, for she initiated new programs and new social services that were sorted out from many religious, philosophical and moral abstract thought and discussion sessions. She got a good look at the extremes of both types, and she was beginning to see the factor of psychological type herself.

> A Settlement is above all a place for enthusiasm, a spot to which those who have a passion for the equalizations of human joys and opportunities are attracted. It is this type of mind which is in itself so often obnoxious to the man of conquering business faculty, to whom the practical world of affairs seems so supremely rational that he would never vote to change the type of it even if he could. The man of social enthusiasm is to him an annoyance and an affront. He does not like to hear him talk and considers him *per se* "unsafe." Such a business man would admit, as an abstract proposition, that society is susceptible to modification and would even agree that all human institutions imply progressive development, but at the same time he deeply distrusts those who seek to reform existing conditions. There is a certain common-sense foundation for this distrust, for too often the reformer is the rebel who defies things as they are, because of the restraints which they impose upon his individual desires rather than because of the general defects of the system. When such a rebel poses for a reformer, his shortcomings are heralded to the world to those who refuse to worship "the god of things as they are."[20]

The first ray and the fourth ray type of mind are once again fairly well delineated here. On the one hand we have a "passion for the equalizations of human joys and opportunities", a "social enthusiasm" for "progressive development," which negatively becomes the defiant rebel who is more concerned with his own personal condition than the general good. On the other hand, we have the "conquering business faculty" that considers the rebel "obnoxious" and "unsafe", views the "practical world of affairs" as being "supremely rational," and "distrusts those who seek to reform existing conditions." Jane Addams had a foot in both camps, for she herself was the enthusiastic reformer, who necessarily had to look into the future and deal with abstractions, but she was predominantly the practical minded person understanding the "business faculty" and the "world of affairs." She never seemed to quite understand those who were predominantly focussed in the world of feeling, of sensitivity, of meaning and abstraction.

> And yet as I recall the members of this early club [Hull-House Social Science], even those who talked the most and the least rationally, seem to me to have been particularly kindly and "safe." The most pronounced anarchist among them has long since become a convert to a religious sect, holding Buddhistic tenets which imply little food and a distrust of all action; he has become a wraith of his former self but he still retains his kindly smile.[21]

The point Jane Addams seems to be making here is that the "type of mind" that one may find enthusiastically and irrationally advocating social change tends to be considered "unsafe" and "obnoxious" to the man of "conquering business faculty." But, viewing the matter over a longer period of time (20 years), Jane Addams found that there was a safe and profound kindliness beneath the irrational talk. One wonders, however, what Jane Addams truly thought of the anarchist turned Buddhist if he was now merely a shadow or ghost of his former self, retaining but a kindly smile. The "distrust of all action" must have appeared ludicrous to her. (We might paranthetically add, however, that the Buddha did not advocate no action, nor excessive action, but right action.)

Insensitive Rules and Regulations. One of the institutions established at Hull-House was a "relief station," which gave food and clothing to the unemployed family. To maintain a just distribution of their limited resources, however, certain rules and regulations had to be drawn up. Of a shipping clerk who had come to the relief station four or five times Jane Addams wrote:

> I told him one day of the opportunity for work on the drainage canal and intimated that if any employment were obtainable, he

ought to exhaust that possibility before asking for help. The man replied that he had always worked indoors and that he could not endure outside work in winter. I am grateful to remember that I was too uncertain to be severe, although I held to my instructions. He did not come again for relief, but worked for two days digging on the canal, where he contracted pneumonia and died a week later. I never lost trace of the two little children he left behind him, although I cannot see them without a bitter consciousness that it was at their expense I learned that life cannot be administered by definite rules and regulations; that wisdom to deal with a man's difficulties comes only through some knowledge of his life and habits as a whole; and that to treat an isolated episode is almost sure to invite blundering.[22]

"Life cannot be administered by definite rules and regulations"—a difficult lesson for many first ray types. But rules and regulations are needed if anarchic chaos is to be avoided. Rules and regulations are most necessary in order to maintain a functioning institution. A love-wisdom is apparently needed in order to continually refine the rules as knowledge and sensitivities expand. Continually finer differentiations are required in order to prevent a structure that crystallizes into rigidity and no longer serves the original purposes.

More Service Activities. In trying to meet the immediate need of the poor in the community, Jane Addams and her co-workers found themselves "spending many hours in efforts to secure support for deserted women, insurance for bewildered widows, damages for injured operators, furniture from the clutches of the installment store. The Settlement is valuable as an information and interpretation bureau. It constantly acts between the various institutions of the city and the people for whose benefit these institutions were erected. The hospitals, the county agencies, and State asylums are often but vague rumors to the people who need them most."[23]

Many of Jane Addams' clients might have had difficulty in gaining information and dealing with various service institutions due to a lack of reading ability, language ability, intellectual ability, etc. But with many who need to or are forced to deal with the institutions of our society, difficulties do ensue not due to level of intelligence or familiarity with the culture, but due to type. Certain information is needed as to services available and as to the necessary procedure to obtain the services. Also a certain *attitude* or *type of energy* is needed in order to secure the information or to deal facilely with the institution. What *is not* needed is an overly friendly attitude, an impatient pleading, the desire for a quick and thorough solution, an emotional appeal or even a moral appeal. What *is* needed is a patient and calm persistence, an impersonality, an ability to state and to hear fact and to take one small but secure step at a time.

An incident comes to mind of a young man who applied for unemployment compensation when his seasonal job came to an end. After collecting the unemployment insurance for a couple of weeks, he was questioned by the clerk as to whether or not he had been actively seeking employment. After some hesitation, the young man explained that he was hand-crafting some wood toys that he might be able to sell in the near future. The clerk said nothing at all to him at that time. When he returned two weeks later, however, the clerk informed him that he, according to his own statement, was self-employed in a toy manufacturing business and therefore was not eligible for unemployment compensation.

What actually occurred? The young man was apparently unconscious of the rules, regulations and guidelines of the particular institution that necessarily limits its services in the effort to prevent fraud and abuse. The young man did not "hear" the fact within the question and did not respond with fact directly to the question. The question was: Are you seeking employment? His response unwittingly and in effect was: I am self-employed. The young man, however, was trying to impart something else. His explanation was a quiet *plea* that his own *personal* case be understood. He was saying something to the effect that he was putting his time and the money to good use by making a good little product. And that this activity was actually *better* than seeking employment. He felt that it was better and, if the clerk was sensitive, the clerk would see that it was better, and the rules and regulations could be adjusted with an understanding wink of the eye. To pretend that he was seeking employment would be a sham. He preferred to be *honest*, to reveal his "heart" on the matter. *If* things went well, he might never have to seek the seasonal unemployment insurance again. He was dealing with subtle moral questions, with conditional "ifs," with nuances of meaning, rather than the concrete documentable facts of the present. His appeal stated that his toy making was not at the manufacturing level but at the hobby level, and that he was actively seeking employment, giving specific names and addresses. He was learning how to communicate with institutions, though not an easy matter for his fourth ray mind.

Jane Addams approached the institution in a different way. Hull-House and the neighboring area was constantly surrounded by the "foul smells of the stockyards and the garbage dumps."[24] The people at Hull-House combated the problem in various ways. First of all they established a small incinerator at Hull-House. They repeatedly reported the condition in the ward to city hall. And they arranged talks for immigrants, pointing out that sweeping refuse out into the streets might work in a rural community from which the immigrants had come but could cause the death of one's children in an urban environment. None of the measures, however, penetrated very far towards the solution of the problem. The next thing that the Hull-House residents did was to begin a "systematic investigation of the city system of garbage collection, both as to its efficiency in other wards and its possible connection with the death rate in the various wards of the city."[25] It was found that the death rate was the highest in the congested foreign colonies. During August and September of a particular year Hull-House reported to the health department 1037 violations of the laws pertaining to the refuse problem. Nothing was done, however, and the death rate remained high.

"In sheer desperation, the following spring when the city contracts were awarded for the removal of garbage, with the backing of two well-known business men, I put in a bid for the garbage removal of the nineteenth ward. My paper was thrown out on a technicality but the incident induced the mayor to appoint me the garbage inspector of the ward." She got up very early in the morning to make sure the men got to work on time, followed wagons to the dump, insisted that the contractor "increase the number of wagons from nine to thirteen and from thirteen to seventeen, although he assured me that he lost money on every one and that the former inspector had let him off with seven."[26]

28

Through her persistent efforts the cleanliness of the neighborhood was greatly improved, and the death rate "dropped from third to seventh in the list of city wards."[27] But the battle did not end there. Apparently, those who opposed her could not dislodge her from her civil service position, so they found a way of eliminating the position altogether. An alderman introduced legislation into the city council that combined the inspection of refuse collection with that of street maintenance, thus forming one position where previously there had been two. Short as her term was, nevertheless she succeeded in leaving her mark and raising the standards.

Dealing with institutions and administrating her own institution was not a peripheral matter but a central focus of her life. This was true also of Gandhi and William Allen White (though not necessarily true of all first ray minds). Van Gogh had a very difficult time understanding the business institution (art gallery and book business), and also the educational and religious institutions with which he was briefly employed. The acute sensitivity and idealistic aspirations of his strong fourth and sixth ray equipment seemed to eclipse any possibility of a first or seventh ray understanding of institutional matters.

The fifth ray mind generally tends, as a path of least resistance, to focus on the factor of knowledge rather than on the procedural matters necessary to institutionalize knowledge. An incident comes to mind of a resident physician at a hospital who refused to take the required yearly chest x-ray—a decision based on the latest scientific knowledge. Thinking of how this stance might benefit others as well, I inquired of the physician just exactly how such policies were formed and changed within the hierarchical administrative structure of the hospital. The response was vague, evasive and incomplete. He simply did not know and apparently was not interested in learning about administrative procedure. For him action followed immediately upon the latest scientific knowledge. Institutions, however, generally tend not to function in that way. In *Esoteric Psychology* it is pointed out that there is a "static stabilizing tendency" to the first ray[28] (at the personaility level), which suggests a juxtaposition of positive and negative factors. "Static" is the negative factor, suggesting a reluctance to change, which tends to result sooner or later in a rigid and crystallized state of affairs. On the other hand, the first ray also tends to bring about a stabilizing condition, which is to say that every new piece of knowledge that presents itself is not immediately implemented. Some time is allowed to see which new ideas gain in strength and which ones die out. In some cases this may mean slower but surer growth. With Jane Addams, however, it was not so much a case of a new piece of knowledge as a whole new set of principles. Her ideas centered around the principles of selfless service, indicative of the level of consciousness attributable to the soul or higher self, whereas the ideas of those in Chicago's City Government during that time emanated primarily from the self-centered personality, manipulating to get the best possible personal advantage. A power struggle necessarily ensued.

The Arts at Hull-House. Many artistic endeavors were undertaken at Hull-House, including poetry readings, music lessons, dramatic presentations, craft projects, etc. One of the first projects undertaken was an art exhibit, which was "surprisingly well attended." According to Jane Addams, the value of the paintings to the neighborhood "had to be determined by each of us according to the value he attached to beauty and the escape it offers from dreary reality into the realm of the imagination."[29] Are paintings merely an imaginative escape, or was she failing to appreciate a subtle matter more accessible to those on the fourth ray of beauty and harmony? Also, it is interesting to note the phrase "dreary reality", which implies that there is a non-reality to "beauty" and to the "realm of the imagination" and that the social problems she encountered on a daily basis constituted the totality of the real world. One could say that the social problems of Chicago or of the industrial revolution were the result of the imagination and dreams put into plans and action of a great many entrepreneurs and politicians. A certain amount of hardship, chaos and inhuman conditions accompanied these manifested ideas due perhaps to the fact that much of the planning was contrary to or unaligned with reality. In other words, was she dealing with "dreary reality" or was she dealing with the results of man's illusions? To put it another way, there is something unreal about this "dreary reality." But there is also something real about it.

The first ray type may have a tendency to limit reality to the economic-survival-power questions. Are the arts a decorative adornment upon the "real world" or are they a necessity of life dealing not with physical survival but with psychological survival and growth? Each ray type as well as each individual tends to see reality in a "refracted" way, resulting in a certain "color distortion." Some of the pronounced types along the two-four-six line have an entirely different view of reality, as we shall see in the cases of van Gogh and Thoreau.

When "life pressed hard in many directions" and when the "stern aspects" of life occupied most of their concerns, it is "rather interesting," wrote Jane Addams, that the first building custom designed for the Hull-House organization was an art gallery. The second floor contained a spacious room "carefully designed and lighted for art exhibits, which had to do with the cultivation of that which appealed to the powers of enjoyment as over against a wage-earning capacity."[30] "The powers of enjoyment"—a strange phrase, indeed. She was certainly adept at dealing with administrative responsibilities and power struggles, but she was never able to penetrate very far into the world of art. (Again, however, there are a great many exceptions to these general tendencies due in part to other ray and also environmental influences.) Art to her was an enjoyment, a pleasant diversion from the sterner and more real aspects of life. It was something you *like*, something that merely creates a little pleasant emotional sensation. There is a tendency to belittle or to view superficially that which lies outside of one's ray penetration. This recalls to mind Thomas Huxley's statement to the clergyman that the idea of immortality could be reduced to *nothing but a likeable idea*. So it seems on the surface of things. The anarchist might say that government is *nothing but* the suppression of the people, therefore, we ought to eliminate government altogether. Or the religious artist might say that science is *nothing but* gadgetry and succeeds only in enmeshing us deeper in materialism instead of getting us closer to truth. Superficial, reductionistic judgements, indeed.

It is also interesting to note that Jane Addams attempted somehow to contrast in a polarizing way art and "the powers of enjoyment" over and against "a wage-earning capacity", implying that money is the measure of all things and that art is peripheral to the real world of money and the market place. Thoreau's wage-earning capacity was, out of choice, at the subsistence level. Had he spent his life increasing his "wage-earning capacity", he would not have been such a rich man. The books he wanted to write were not those the public wanted to buy—until long after his death.

Expansion of Work into Political Areas. Jane Addams and some of the residents at Hull-House continued to refine and increase their political efficacy. In 1895 the Mayor of Chicago appointed Jane Addams to serve on a commission to investigate conditions in the county poorhouse. She was thirty-five years old at the time. Mrs. Florence Kelley, a resident at Hull-House, gathered statistical information on Chicago's industrial condition and presented it to the Illinois State Bureau of Labor. The matter was then investigated by a special committee of the Illinois Legislature. "As a result of its investigation, this committee recommended to the Legislature the provisions which afterward became those of the first factory law of Illinois, regulating the sanitary conditions of the sweatshop and fixing fourteen as the age at which a child might be employed."[31]

Statistical documentation was presented to the appropriate units of power. Further pressure had to be applied in terms of lobbying. "I remember I very much disliked the word and still more the prospect of lobbying itself, and we insisted that well-known Chicago women should accompany this first little group of Settlement fold who with trade unionists moved upon the state capitol in behalf of factory legislation."[32] Who accompanied their lobbying efforts was also an important power factor. Women who had power and influence in the community were asked to join them.

Other efforts of theirs included the attempt to prohibit the sale of cocaine to minors, which brought them into conflict with several druggists. "I recall an Italian druggist living on the edge of the neighborhood, who finally came with a committee of his fellow countrymen to see what Hull-House wanted of him, thoroughly convinced that no such effort could be disinterested."[33] After long effort, a new law regulating its sale was finally obtained in 1907.

Jane Addams participated in the problems of settling disputes between labor and management, and she did this at a time when arbitration was in its infancy and at a time when both parties were prone to resort to violence. After the Pullman strike she participated in a convention of Industrial Conciliation and Arbitration which was arranged by "various elements in the community . . . unexpectedly brought together that they might soberly consider and rectify the weaknesses in the legal structure which the strike revealed."[34] As a result of their efforts, the Illinois legislature passed a law creating a State Board of Conciliation and Arbitration.

A long list of social service activities could be added to this brief survey of the life of Jane Ãddams. She served as a member of the Chicago Board of Education. She maintained three baths in the basement of Hull-House, since the tenements were without baths, and argued successfully for the building of the first public bathhouse in Chicago. She persuaded the Public Library Board to establish a branch reading room at Hull-House. A dramatic arts club was established at Hull-House, putting on plays by Shaw, Ibsen, Galsworthy and others. She arranged for college extension classes to be held at Hull-House, and at its peak the faculty numbered thirty-five. In 1909 she became the first woman president of the National Conference of Charities and Corrections, now the National Conference of Social Welfare. She led in the fight to give women the vote and was an ardent pacifist. She served as president of the Women's International League for Peace and Freedom, was the chairperson of the Woman's Peace Party, and in 1931 she was awarded the Nobel peace prize.

Summary.   There is a tendency among many who have first ray minds to have an interest in science but to lack the "zeal" or the capability of going into sufficient depth to carve out a career in a scientific field. In her twenties Jane Addams came to a point where she could cling to only one thing and that was the "desire to live in a really living world," rejecting any "shadowy intellectual reflection of it." She felt that "lumbering our minds with literature" was an interference with right conduct and practical action. In art she preferred the "human documents" of Albrecht Dürer to the imaginative, idyllic scenes of beauty and harmony. She identified with young people who "feel nervously the need of putting theory into practice." Generally speaking, the first ray mind tends to be attracted to the "really vital situation spread before our eyes" and tends to want to put "theory into practice" and to do something about the concrete situation. In the case of Jane Addams this demonstrated as an urge and an ability to institutionalize a great variety of social service programs. Frequently, with individuals who have first ray minds, there tends to be a mental-physical alignment or interplay and a negation or control of the emotional factor. In contrast to this, many fourth ray minds tend to aspire to an intuitive-emotion alignment and interplay. As a result, the fourth ray type may bring a needed sensitivity and insight into a particular situation but may tend to be vague or neglectful regarding physical plane detail.

Frequently, one will find the first ray type dealing with the acute or emergency situation, requiring as it does immediate practical action. Qualities of the first ray exhibited in this regard may be poise, a presence of mind, detachment and impersonality. Generally speaking, the fourth ray type with its tendency towards abstraction, sensitivity and identification with the suffering person, tends not to be attracted to emergency work, although the drama of conflict may have its attraction for the fourth ray type during certain stages of development. Other rays influencing the individual through his various "bodies" can offset the ray of the mental body. Statistical studies of the first ray differ from scientific studies in that scientific studies deal in greater depth with cause and effect and with those elements that are true for all time (principles, natural laws). The statistical studies of the first ray type are concerned with the documentation of a present and politically significant condition. The two areas do overlap. The fourth ray type is generally not attracted to studies of a statistical nature. Money comes more under the domain of rays one, three and seven than it does under rays two, four and six. Money deals more with the immediate, vital, political and concrete situation than it does with the abstract realms.

Jane Addams' interpretation of the life of Christ placed emphasis on "the will" and "action." She rejected the "religious consciousness" in favor of a "simple acceptance of Christ's message" that sought humanitartian expression in social organisms. She also rejected the "abstract mind" given over to "discussion", "propaganda" and "speculation", while appreciating the "concrete minds" and "men of affairs" who demonstrate "actual attainment." In her argument she seemed to be substantiating a point of view more indicative of a first ray mind, while looking superficially at the fourth ray type that frequently likes to discuss abstract matters but may be slow to act and to institutionalize. To the "conquering business faculty" that deals with the "rational", practical affairs of the world, the fourth ray type may appear to be impractical, too idealistic, and "unsafe." Jane Addams recalled to mind a "most pronounced anarchist" who eventually became a Buddhist and one that distrusted all action—a point of view that tends to find little sympathy among first ray types. A difficult lesson for Jane Addams and for many first ray types is that "life cannot be administered by definite rules and regulations." Life certainly cannot be administered *without* rules and regulations, but something more, perhaps the wisdom to deal with the whole, is needed.

There tends to be a "static stabilizing tendency" to the first ray. The static tendency may cause crystallization or a rigid inflexibility; "stabilizing" suggests a condition where every new piece of knowledge that presents itself is not immediately implemented. Some time is allowed to see which new ideas gain in strength and which ones die out. In some cases this may mean slower but surer growth.

Jane Addams saw art as primarily an "escape from dreary reality." The first ray type may tend to limit reality to the economic-survival-power questions and may tend to view the arts as a pleasurable escape. "Wage-earning capacity" may seem then of greater value than a mere "enjoyment." There is a tendency to belittle or to view superficially that which lies outside of one's ray penetration.

REFERENCE NOTES TO CHAPTER II

1. Jane Addams, *Twenty Years at Hull-House with Autobiographical Notes* (New York: The Macmillan Company, 1910), pp. 62-63.
2. Ibid., pp. 65-66.
3. Ibid., p. 64.
4. Ibid., pp. 67-68.
5. Ibid., pp. 70-71.
6. Ibid., p. 75.
7. Ibid., p. 85.
8. Ibid., p. 122.
9. Ibid., p. 89.
10. Ibid., pp. 101, 102, 103, 104.
11. Ibid., pp. 107, 109.
12. Ibid., p. 110.
13. Ibid., p. 98.
14. Ibid., p. 132.
15. Ibid., p. 133.
16. Ibid., p. 150.
17. Ibid., p. 122.
18. Ibid., pp. 123-4.
19. Ibid., pp. 192-3.
20. Ibid., p. 184.
21. Ibid., p. 185.
22. Ibid., p. 162.
23. Ibid., p. 167.
24. Ibid., p. 283.
25. Ibid., p. 284.
26. Ibid., pp. 285-6.
27. Ibid., p. 288.
28. Bailey, *Esoteric Psychology*, I, p. 386.
29. Addams, p. 372.
30. Ibid., p. 148.
31. Ibid., p. 201.
32. Ibid., p. 202.
33. Ibid., p. 299.
34. Ibid., p. 213.

Chapter III

Vincent van Gogh: Fourth Ray Mind

Vincent van Gogh was born in the Netherlands in 1853. At the apprenticeship level he explored careers as an art dealer, a teacher, a book dealer, a minister, until 1881 at the age of twenty-eight he devoted all his energies to the field of art. Supported by his brother Theo, Vincent felt pressed to achieve success as a painter. At the same time, however, he uncompromisingly refused to cater to any commercial or traditional interests and strove to develop his art along lines that satisfied his own sensitivities. In 1890 after a brief but intense nine years of painting and after producing what have come to be known as great works of art, he ended his own life at the age of thirty-seven.

Rays and the Planes. There is a tendency for those with fourth ray minds to be more emotionally sensitive or more feeling conscious than those with first or fifth ray minds. This is certainly not always the case due to several other salient factors (level of development, rays of other bodies, astrological and environmental factors). The first ray mind tends toward a mental-physical alignment, which expesses itself as practicality, emotional control or inhibition, and getting the physical plane into a functioning order, as we have seen somewhat in the case of Jane Addams. Emotion from one point of view tends to interfere with power, with control, with poise and impersonality. It tends to interfere with the presence of mind that demands quick and right decisions in the minor and major emergencies of the present. The fifth ray mind generally relies on reasoning and observation and tends to distrust feeling. Emotion tends to disturb clarity of thought. This is generally evident in the pronounced fifth ray type but may not be clearly evident when the two-four-six line is also a strongly conditioning factor.

The major ray of the physical or seventh plane is the seventh ray. The ray of the emotional or sixth plane is the sixth ray. The ray of the mental or fifth plane is the fifth ray. And the ray of the intuitional or fourth plane is the fourth ray. Thus, the scientific or fifth ray type finds its "home" on the fifth plane of mind. The first ray type finds a path of least resistance to the seventh or physical plane. And the fourth ray type finds affinity with the sixth plane of emotion and also the fourth plane of intuition. (See *Esoteric Psychology*, I, p. 51, for an enumeration of the planes and the rays.) As a result, the fourth ray type of mind may tend to lack sharp analysis when it comes to the physical form (inaccuracy in detail or in form). The fourth ray mind may tend to attune itself to subtlety of feeling, as it mirrors or strives to link with the intuition. This type of sensitive-aspirational-intuitive endeavor tends to find greater expression in the arts, generally speaking, than it does, say, in political organization and the sciences. The sensitive-intuitive factor is an asset, however, in all fields, and the fourth ray can be of benefit in a wide range of endeavors in conjunction with other rays. On the mental plane the fourth ray mind may tend to be not as clearly logical nor as dependent on reasoning as are both the first and particularly the fifth ray minds. The hunch, the fine feeling for things and later the intuitive grasp of matters tend to play a greater role than do the patient, painstaking scrutinizing of every observable detail and the clear reasoning from every thinkable angle.

Strong Passions—"Highest Pitch of Enthusiasm." In his early twenties Vincent wrote to his brother Theo: "I have a more or less irresistible passion for books, and I continually want to instruct myself, to study if you like, just as much as I want to eat my bread. . . . When I was in other surroundings, in the surroundings of pictures and works of art, you know how I had a violent passion for them, reaching the highest pitch of enthusiasm."[1] Instead of distrusting or cautiously observing his passions and enthusiasms, van Gogh was using them as a sort of guide. The "highest pitch of enthusiasm" is indicative of a mind more mystically than practically oriented. This suggests the strong possibility of a fourth ray mind in combination with a sixth ray emotional body striving for some transcendent or ideal state of consciousness. "Strong passions" is given as one of the vices of the fourth ray type in *Esoteric Psychology*, I (p. 206).

Strong Affections—"Tone and Mood"—At-One-Ment.

> I had a long talk with Harry until late in the evening, about all kinds of things, about the Kingdom of God and about the Bible; we walked up and down the station platform, talking thus, and I think we shall never forget those last moments before we said good-by. We know each other so well: his work was my work; the people he knows there, I know also; his life was my life. It was given me to look so deeply into the family's history because I love them, less because I know the particulars of that history than because I feel the tone and mood of their life and character. We walked up and down the platform in that commonplace world, but with emotions far beyond it. Such moments do not last long and soon we had to part.[2]

We find here not information or knowledge or fact, but mood, feeling and sensitivity. We also find strong affection and love. ("Strong affections" are given as one of the virtues of the fourth ray type, *Eso. Psycho.*, p. 205.) It is interesting that van Gogh felt that he *knew* the family, not through the particulars of the family history, but through feeling the "tone and mood of their life and character." There is a tendency for the fourth ray mind to emphasize the kind of knowing that occurs through the feeling nature or through love (the heart), rather than the kind that occurs through the brain and intellect. The particulars of the form nature were incidental; he knew him because "his life was my life", because there was a sense of common experience, intimate involvement, at-one-ment. In this regard it is interesting that the emotional and intuitive planes (sixth and fourth) are planes of unity, whereas the physical and mental planes (seventh and fifth) are planes of separation. From the scientific point of view the type of knowing that comes through tone and mood is definitely suspect and on questionable grounds. The scientific method depends much on detached observation, not intimacy of tone and mood. Van Gogh greatly emphasized one and neglected or even rejected the other. The physical or form world was to him "that commonplace world", so short of the ideal; he was concerned with "emotions far beyond it." His paintings convey the same preference: the feeling, the tone and mood of a landscape predominate and not accuracy of form. The fourth ray "is pre-eminently the ray of colour, of the artist whose colour is always great, though his drawing will often be defective."[3]

Picturesque Word-Painting, Exaggeration. Van Gogh described an illness he had in the following terms:

> I had been ill: my mind was tired; my soul disillusioned; and my body, suffering. I whom God has endowed at least with moral energy and a strong instinct for affection—I fell into an abyss of the most bitter discouragement, and with horror I felt a deadly poison penetrate my smothered heart. I spent three months on the moors, you know that beautiful region where the soul retires within itself and enjoys a delicious rest, when everything breathes calm and peace; where the soul, in the presence of God's immaculate creation, throws off the yoke of conventions, forgets society and loosens its bonds with the strength of renewed youth; where every thought forms a prayer, where everything that is not in harmony with fresh, free nature disappears from the heart. Oh, there the tired souls find rest, there the exhausted man regains his youthful strength. So I passed my days of illness . . .[4]

We are learning little of fact about van Gogh's illness. We are learning again about "mood and tone", about his emotional world that mirrors in its highest moments something of a mystical or transcendent state of being. Once again there is inaccuracy and exaggeration: "I felt a deadly poison penetrate my smothered heart." Also characteristic of the fourth ray type is a fluctuation between extremes—the overactive *rajas* (activity) and the underactive *tamas* (inertia). Van Gogh went from "the most bitter discouragement" to that "beautiful region where the soul . . . enjoys a delicious rest" and "where every thought forms a prayer." The fourth ray type may have to struggle with a dramatic imbalance of extremes particularly during youth. Van Gogh recognized his endowment of "moral energy and a strong instinct for affection"—once again emphasizing dramatically a sentient or feeling consciousness. Some of the "virtues to be acquired" by the fourth ray type are "serenity, self-control and accuracy",[5] which replace the fluctuating moods, the loss of control through excessive feeling, the exaggeration and extravagance.

Education, Religion, Language, Art. Vincent van Gogh as a young man was apprenticed as an art dealer in his uncle's firm first at The Hague, then London and finally Paris. He was dismissed when he was twenty-three years old. He became a teacher at a boys boarding school in England. He gave that up to prepare for exams that would enable him to study theology. But the difficult bookish or academic learning on matters that did not seem to relate to the spirit of religion, which is what he wanted to bring to the people, forced him to quit this study. He attended a three month school of evangelization at Brussels and got a temporary six months position at Wesmes where he gave Bible classes, taught children and visited the sick. Because of unconventional behavior, his position was not renewed. He had also worked for a short time at a book store, but instead of learning the business he was found translating the Bible into French, German and English from the Dutch text. In his late twenties with arrangements with his brother Theo for temporary support, he settled into a career in art. Unable to sell any paintings, however, his brother's support extended until Vincent's death.

Many fourth ray minds are attracted to these fields of endeavor—religion, languages, art, education—although, needless to say, all the types are to be found in these broad fields. Business, generally speaking, is less attractive to the fourth ray type, which was certainly true in the case of van Gogh, but there are a great many exceptions to this tendency. Many times, for example, one will find fourth ray minds in small businesses that are craft related. One may also find them employed in large businesses for their special skills, but rarely will one find them at any complex level of management and administration.

Of van Gogh at the book store it was said that he "could not be trusted to serve the public . . . except perhaps to sell a quire of letter paper or a half penny print once in a while. For he had not the slightest knowledge of the book trade, and he did not make any attempt to learn." When he was supposed to give customers information about prints, "he paid no attention to his employer's interests, but said explicitly and unreservedly what he thought of their artistic value. Once more: he was unfit for business."[6] Part of van Gogh's lack of fitness for business can be attributed to his youth, to his emotional instability and part can be attributed to ray type. Van Gogh was concerned primarily about the "artistic value" of a print, whereas the owners were concerned about meeting the customers' wants and about selling merchandise. His refined artistic sensitivity enabled him to see things that other people did not, and he apparently felt an impelling obligation to point them out. In an educational setting it might be more appropriate to speak "explicitly and unreservedly" about the artistic value of a print, but in a business setting one is dealing less with "meaning" and more with "things concrete." The refinement in business goes along with an entirely different line of service and activity.

The Heart, Identification.   Upon reading *Of the Imitation of Christ* Vincent wrote to his brother Theo: "Thomas á Kempis' book is peculiar; in it are words so profound and serious that one cannot read them without emotion, almost fear—at least if one reads with a sincere desire for light and truth—the language has an eloquence which wins the heart because it comes from the heart."[7] Again we see Vincent proceeding along the line of sensitivity to meaning and not at all along the line of social action or scientific knowledge—bearing in mind, however, that although starkly divergent at some levels, these ways overlap, integrate and blend with one other. The words of Thomas á Kempis inspired "emotion, almost fear" and they won "the heart." The words "emotion" and "heart" can refer to a very wide range of sensations, experiences and states of consciousness.

If we differentiate between head (intellect) and heart (feeling-sensitivity), then, generally speaking, the fourth ray mind may tend towards heart-feeling while the first and fifth ray minds may tend towards head-intellect. This we have noted in respect to the planes. In van Gogh's case "the heart" was particularly emphasized not only due to a fourth ray mind (and sixth ray emotional body) but also due to the two-four-six line conditioning either the personality or soul or possibly both. It is most difficult to say from his writings alone, but it is possible that either the soul or personality was on the sixth ray of idealism and devotion. There seems to be also a possibility that not only the mind but also the personality was on the fourth ray of harmony through conflict. In either case we have a sensitive, mystical inclination, a person who loves to delve into philosophical and/or religious abstractions, who holds

42

tenaciously to certain discovered truths, and who has a difficult time with mental disciplines and physical practicality. When a fourth ray mind is working in conjunction with a first or seventh ray personality, then discipline and practicality, even organizational and administrative work, will more likely be evidenced. It is clear that van Gogh had a fourth ray mind, but not all fourth ray minds exhibit his pronounced characteristics.

The heart qualities and the ability to identify with other living creatures were carried to an extreme in van Gogh. A pastor from Borinage where van Gogh was an evangelist stated: "The family with whom he had boarded told me that every time he found a caterpillar on the ground in the garden, he carefully picked it up and took it to a tree. Apart from this trait, which perhaps will be considered insignificant or even foolish, I have retained the impression that Vincent van Gogh was actuated by a high ideal: self-forgetfulness and devotion to all other beings was the guiding principle which he accepted wholeheartedly."[8] Van Gogh clearly lacked knowledge. From a scientific point of view it was, indeed, a foolish gesture. On the other hand, other types when pronounced in their specialized directions and lacking in a holistic balance, can readily appear foolish along different lines.

Conflict with Administrative Coldness and Red Tape.

I must tell you that with evangelists it is the same as with artists. There is an old academic school, often detestable, tyrannical, the accumulation of horrors, men who wear a cuirass, a steel armor, of prejudices and conventions; when these people are in charge of affairs, they dispose of positions, and by a system of red tape they try to keep their proteges in their places and to exclude the other man. Their God is like the God of Shakespeare's drunken Falstaff, *le dedans d'une église* the inside of a church; indeed, by a curious chance some of these evangelical (???) gentlemen find themselves with the same point of view on spiritual things as that drunken character (perhaps they would be somewhat surprised to discover this if they were capable of human emotions?). But there is little fear of their blindness ever changing to clearsightedness in such matters.

This state of affairs has its bad side for him who does not agree, but protests against it with all his soul and all his heart and all the indignation of which he is capable. For my part I respect academicians who are not like these, but the respectable ones are

rarer than one would first believe. One of the reasons why I am unemployed now, why I have been unemployed for years, is simply
that I have different ideas than the gentlemen who give the places
to men who think as they do. It is not merely the question of dress
which they have hypocritically reproached me with; it is a much
more serious question, I assure you.[9]

Several conflicts are suggested here: the generation conflict
between the old and the young, the conflict between established
convention and innovation, between personality self-
centeredness and soul inclusiveness, and there is also the conflict between the first and fourth ray type. It is interesting to
note the characteristics of the "old academic school," the people
"in charge of affairs," that van Gogh particularly criticized. He
accused them of wearing "a steel armor," in other words, as being cold and impenetrable, inflexible, lacking, perhaps in
warmth, sympathy and understanding. He complained of their
system of "red tape" and their hiring practices that were
political and not based on merit. He felt that they were not
"capable of human emotions" and thus insensitive. He accused
them of being "tyrannical" or, in other words, of misusing
power. These characteristics for the most part are the negative
attributes of the first ray type—although we are getting a distorted picture through van Gogh's own inability to understand
and appreciate the work of the first ray. The accusations
"detestable . . . the accumulation of horrors . . . blindness" testify
only to exaggeration and lack of accuracy. To become an
evangelist there was the need to have academic knowledge of
religious doctrine acquired through scholastic discipline, to
have some understanding of how to administrate a small institution and of the hierarchical power structure involved, and
to have something of the spirit of the teaching that inspires and
gives of itself in service to others. Van Gogh was sufficiently en-
dowed with the latter, but he did not recognize and appreciate
the value and place of the other two.

Knowledge of the rays throws a great deal of new light on
these age-old conflicts and can do much to alleviate them. In the
area of creativity, innovation and the sensing of important new
directions the intuitively inclined fourth ray mind makes an invaluable contribution. Innovation and meaningful change keep
an institution alive in the sense of having a growing and
developing consciousness. There are institutions that, although

able to sustain themselves materially, are rigid, dogmatic and crystallized and thus in a state of decomposition and decay as viewed from the consciousness and spiritual point of view. On the other hand, creating and maintaining an institution requires a great deal of sacrifice and discipline and responsibility that the fourth ray mind, particularly the youthful one, may have a tendency to overlook.

"Fine Sentiment" More Than Definition.

Since the Reverend . . . translated Goethe's *Faust,* Father and Mother have read that book, for now that a clergyman has translated it, it cannot be so very immoral??? . . . But they consider it nothing but the fatal consequences of an ill-timed love. . . - Now take Mauve [a fellow artist], for instance. When he reads something that is deep, he does not say at once, That man means this or that. For poetry is so deep and intangible that one cannot define everything systematically. But Mauve has a fine sentiment, and, you see, I think that sentiment worth so much more than definitions and criticism.[10]

The scientific mind would generally not be inclined to say that "fine sentiment" is worth more than definitions. On the contrary, the developed fifth ray mind relies heavily on precise definition. Van Gogh, on the other hand, valued most highly a certain "fine sentiment" that enables one to perceive something that is "deep and intangible." The intellect is involved with clear definition, which is a process of isolation and separation. The "fine sentiment" used to discern the "deep and intangible" involves the feeling-intuitive interplay. There is no reason why both intellect and fine feeling cannot be used in the effort to arrive at intuitive knowledge. Fine feeling can be highly valuable in scientific work, and precise definition can also be highly valuable in the more abstract disciplines.

To Write Freely—Not Dry and Concise.
Vincent inquired of his brother Theo in what manner he should write: "Do you want me to write in a kind of business style, dry and correct and weighing and carefully choosing my words—and, in fact, not saying anything; or do you want me to continue writing about everything the way I have lately, telling you the thoughts that come into my mind, without being afraid of letting myself go,

without keeping back my thoughts or censoring them? The latter is what I should like best, that is, to write freely, saying exactly what I mean."[11] On the one hand we have a "business style, dry and correct" and a careful weighing and choosing of words, and on the other hand we have a "letting myself go," telling the thoughts that come into mind," without any censorship. Both in speech and writing, the first and fifth ray types would be more inclined toward the first method of correctness, careful choosing of words, censorship and dryness, as can generally be noticed in the area of politics, business and science. The fourth ray type would generally tend toward a more spontaneous, colorful, dramatic, truthful expression (truthful in the sense of opening one's heart and mind) in speech and writing. In *Esoteric Psychology* it is stated that the fourth ray type "will generally talk well and have a sense of humour, but he varies between brilliant conversations and gloomy silences, according to his mood."[12] With such factors as mood, humour, dramatic and colorful utterances the feeling nature is evident. With dryness, correctness, etc., the intellect tends to dominate.

In a later correspondence van Gogh again brought up the matter of writing style: "I know that at present many people call everything that is only an interchange of *views*, everything outside of *business* or *facts*, quite superfluous and even nonsensical in a letter, and so they arrive at a very concise form, which, however, is at the same time a rather unsatisfactory, disappointing way of corresponding."[13] From Vincent's point of view of sharing matters close to his heart, the "concise form" is disappointing. Vincent began the above letter with the statement: "Thanks for your letter, though you yourself admit it to be rather short." Theo, a business man, most likely had a first ray mind and felt more comfortable with the "concise form." Vincent wanted very much for his brother to understand him, to believe in his worth, but Vincent did not comprehend his brother's interests. Vincent considered business interests ignoble—far below the lofty sentiments of art—yet Vincent was dependent on his brother for support.

Brother! when you told me the other day, "I think in the matter of finance I am on the trail of a new conception"—what I thought of it was, in short, That's bad enough. I should not have thought so if you had written: In the matter of printing I am on the trail of

46

something, or—I have discovered a number of energetic new artists, with whom I shall probably be able to do business, or something of the sort—in short, if you had discovered something in the field of work or art, I should have thought it excellent, but—the field of finance—pardon my saying it—is too much in the air for my taste.[14]

It is no wonder that Theo—although he did at times try to express himself in the way his brother preferred—reverted back to the "concise form" of the business letter. Printing, that is, the craft aspect of printing, and art were areas Vincent could relate to, but finance, putting it as mildly as he could, was an area he would not even discuss. Generally speaking, areas such as banking, finance, insurance, etc., are comprehended more readily by the first, third and possibly seventh ray types.

During a business recession when Theo did not know if he would be able to hold his position with the firm, let alone finance Vincent's extended apprenticeship, Vincent suggested to him that he give up business and become an artist. Financially, according to Vincent, somehow it would all work out. It was a preposterous projection on Vincent's part, and it illustrates how thoroughly preoccupied with one's own type of endeavor one can be. There is a tendency for some mystically inclined fourth ray minds to look at financial matters in a very impractical way. A less developed fourth ray mind is likely to exhibit more aggressiveness towards a goal of a more material nature (see *Esoteric Psychology*, II, p. 291). Also a fourth ray mind modified by rays one, three or seven will tend to look at financial matters in a more "realistic" or practical fashion.

Vincent wanted to let himself go and "write freely" and did not like the concise business form that dealt mainly with factual matters. When his brother Theo wrote freely, however, discussing such matters as finance, they began to discover that in some respects they were worlds apart. Theo had to revert to the more "consise form."

Friendship. "It is sometimes difficult for me to give up a friendship," wrote Vincent, "but if I go into a studio and have to think, talk about inane things, don't mention anything of importance and don't express your feelings about art—that would make me more melancholy than if I stayed away altogether.

47

Just because I should like to find and keep a real friendship, it is difficult for me to comform to a conventional friendship."[15]

Could Vincent not have maintained an acquaintanceship, a friendship less than the ideal? Did it have to be the extremes of either an ideal, harmonious friendship or no friendship? Could it not have been "conventional", that is, polite and cordial and of some mutual benefit? Of the fourth ray type it is said that he is a "delightful and difficult person to live with" (*Esoteric Psychology*, I, p. 207). When the fourth ray influences at either the personality or mental levels, there may be evidenced the pronounced extremes of harmony, delight and profound mutual understanding on the one hand, and conflict, difficulty and argumentation on the other.

"Dame Nature, Dame Reality." In a letter to a friend and fellow artist, Vincent was able to share matters close to his heart that he was not able to share with his brother Theo: "Rappard, I believe that, though you are working at the academy, you are trying more and more to become a true realist, and that even at the academy you will stick to reality—however, without being conscious of it yourself. Without knowing it, this academy is a mistress who prevents a more serious, a warmer, a more fruitful love from awakening in you. Let this mistress go, and fall desperately in love with your real sweetheart: Dame Nature or Reality . . . She renews, she refreshes, she gives life, this Dame Nature, this Dame Reality."[16]

Among many fourth ray types we find a tendency to view "reality" in less concrete more mystical terms than the other two types. The personification of nature as "your real sweetheart: Dame Nature or Dame Reality" suggests a loving rapport with a living entity, a conscious being, an invisible god, manifesting through the forms of nature. Reality with a capital "R" suggests that the visible reality to which we are accustomed is something far less. Many composers, poets and artists have endeavored down the ages not to define but to hint at or to convey something of the spirit of a transcendent or invisible Reality. This is one way in which the bridging work of the fourth ray (The Link between the Three and the Three, The Divine Intermediary[17]) becomes evident. One can see also a fundamental link between the second ray manifesting through religion and the fourth ray of Beauty and Art.

"A Certain Passion." Though he did not like to define things, without fully realizing it Vincent did endeavor to define subtle matters from time to time: "Though I see, for instance, in the Salon number so many pictures which, if you like, are faultlessly drawn and painted as to technique, yet many of them bore me terribly because they give me neither food for the heart nor the mind, because they have obviously been made without a certain passion."[18]

To van Gogh a true work of art is one made with a "certain passion", a certain fire, and as a result it gives "food for the heart and the mind." One can see that van Gogh clearly considered accuracy of form secondary to something else that he deeply felt and struggled to portray in his art. Although it was 'obvious" to van Gogh that the faultlessly painted pictures as to technique lacked a certain passion, it was not so obvious to others. To Jane Addams, for example, paintings represented an enjoyment and a mere escape from dreary reality. To van Gogh they were food for heart and mind and a means of contacting Reality.

Summary. There is a tendency for those with fourth ray minds to be more emotionally sensitive or more feeling conscious than those with first or fifth ray minds. This is due in part to the interplay and affinity that the fourth ray mind tends to have with the emotional and intuitive planes. The fourth ray type of mind may tend to lack sharp analysis when it comes to the physical form or to forms in general and, therefore, may tend to be vague and inaccurate. The fourth ray mind may tend to attune itself to subtlety of feeling, as it mirrors or strives to link with the intuition. The sensitive-aspirational-intuitive endeavor may tend to find an outlet in some creative art form. On the mental plane the fourth ray mind may tend to be not as clearly logical nor as dependent on reasoning as are the first and particularly the fifth ray minds.

Strong passions and enthusiasms may mark the fourth ray type. The mood, feeling and tone of a situation may be more evident to the fourth ray type than observable fact and detailed information. Strong affections and friendships can also be of special importance to the fourth ray type. From the scientific point of view the type of knowing that comes through "tone and mood" is definitely suspect and on questionable grounds. The scientific method depends more on detached observation, not intimacy of tone and mood. Van Gogh referred to the physical or form world as "that commomplace world" and was concerned with "emotions far beyond it." His paintings display a greater concern for color than for accuracy of form, which tends to be characteristic of the fourth ray type. His writing is also "colorful" in that there is much picturesque word-painting, which often becomes exaggeration. Also characteristic of the fourth ray type is a fluctuation between extremes: "the most bitter discouragement" is turned overnight into a "beautiful region where the soul enjoys a delicious rest and every thought forms a prayer."

As a young man Vincent was attracted to the field of religion, the study of languages, education and art. He "was unfit for business" and he did not seem to have any administrative sense. As well as the fourth ray, it seems that there was much sixth ray present in van Gogh's psychological equipment, certainly at the emotional level and possibly at either the personality or egoic level. The sixth ray in conjunction with the fourth ray may tend to augment a sensitive, mystical inclination and an enjoyment of philosophical or religious abstractions, but may also incline one towards physical impracticality and a difficulty wih mental disciplines. Van Gogh's sensitivity and devotion were at times carried to extremes. As an evangelist his "devotion to all other beings" extended somewhat foolishly to the caterpillar as he aided it from the ground to the tree. To his evangelistic work van Gogh brought the gifts of an enthusiastic religious spirit, self-forgetfulness and a high ideal, but he lacked scholastic discipline and an understanding of administrative procedures. He referred to the old academic school and the people in charge of affairs as being tyrannical, blind, detestable, wearing a steel armor and not capable of human emotions.

According to van Gogh, a certain "fine sentiment" was worth more than definition in the effort to discern the "deep and intangible." In writing to his brother Theo, Vincent preferred a style of "letting oneself go", writing the thoughts as they come to mind, without careful weighing, choosing and censoring. He did not like the dry and correct business style, which he felt was not saying anything at all. Both the speech and writing of the first and fifth ray types would generally tend towards a careful choosing of words, censorship and dryness, as can generally be noticed in the areas of politics, business and science. The fourth ray type would generally tend toward a more spontaneous, colorful, dramatic, and open expression in speech and writing. The fourth ray type "will generally talk well and have a sense of humour, but he varies between brilliant conversations and gloomy silences, according to his mood." With such factors as mood, humour, dramatic and colorful utterances the feeling nature is evident. With dryness, correctness, etc., the intellect tends to dominate.

The world of "finance" made no sense to Vincent at all. Areas such as banking, finance, insurance, etc., tend not to attract the fourth ray type, but when rays one, three or seven are also present in an individual's ray equipment, the fourth ray may be found in those areas. In matters of friendship Vincent was very sensitive to the high ideal and to perfect harmony (six and four), and he tended toward the extremes of a very close friendship or no relationship at all (fourth ray tendency). He disliked the "conventional" friendships or relationships more characteristic of the impersonal first ray types. It is said that the fourth ray type is a "delightful and difficult person to live with."

Van Gogh chose to let the academic of art go for a "more fruitful love", which he called 'Dame Nature or Reality." A strong mystical sense is more likely to be found in one with a fourth ray mind than with the first and fifth ray mental types due to the alignment with the more abstract planes of unity. Van Gogh prefered the art that was made with a certain passion, for it provides food for the heart and mind," rather than technically faultless paintings that do not.

REFERENCE NOTES TO CHAPTER III

1. *The Complete Letters of Vincent van Gogh*, trans. J. van Gogh-Bouger (Greenwich, Connecticut: The New York Graphic Society, 1959), I, p. 194.
2. Ibid., p. 65.
3. Bailey, *Esoteric Psychology*, I p. 207.
4. *Letters*, I, p. 69.
5. Bailey, *Esoteric Psychology*, I, p. 206.
6. *Letters*, I, pp. 109, 113.
7. Ibid., p. 137.
8. Ibid., p. 224.
9. Ibid., pp. 196-7.
10. Ibid., p. 238.
11. Ibid., p. 301.
12. Bailey, *Esoteric Psychology*, I, p. 207.
13. *Letters* II, p. 211.
14. Ibid., p. 215.
15. Ibid, I, p. 540.
16. Ibid., III, pp. 311, 312.
17. Bailey, *Esoteric Psychology*, I, p. 71.
18. *Letters*, II, p. 374.

Chapter IV
Charles Darwin: Fifth Ray Mind

The English naturalist, Charles Darwin (1809-1882), is known primarily for his formulation of the theory of evolution through natural selection. His father, a physician, sent Charles to Edinburgh University to prepare for the medical profession. Charles felt unfitted for the task, however, and after a short time dropped out and went to Christ's College, Cambridge, with the idea of becoming a clergyman. This was said to be the last resort for failures in rich families. During this period he became acquainted with several scientists who encouraged him to pursue his deep interest in natural history.

Charles Darwin, upon receiving a degree, acquired an unpaid position as naturalist on the H.M.S. *Beagle* through the recommendation of a professor of botany. The voyage was the real schooling and preparation for his life's work. From December, 1831, to October, 1836, Darwin sailed on the surveying expedition which visited Cape Verde and other Atlantic Islands, the South American coasts, Galapagos Islands, Tahiti, New Zealand, Australia and several other places. His geological studies were published upon his return. In 1859 his most famous work appeared in print: *The Origin of the Species* in which he formulated the theory of evolution by natural selection. This was followed by several other works including: *The Variations of Animals and Plants Under Domestication* (1868), *Descent of Man* (1871), *The Expression of Emotions in Man and Animals* (1872), *Insectivorous Plants* (1875), and *The Power of Movement in Plants* (1880).

Collecting and Classifying. "By the time I went to day-school," wrote Darwin, "my taste for natural history, and more especially for collecting, was well developed. I tried to make out the names of the plants, and collected all sorts of things, shells, seals, franks, coins, and minerals. The passion for collecting, which leads a man to systematic naturalist, a virtuoso or a miser, was very strong in me, and was clearly innate, as none of my sisters or brothers ever had this taste."[1]

Not all scientific minds have a "passion for collecting" and not all children who like to collect have scientific minds, but the tendency to collect and classify various things in childhood may indicate a budding scientific mind, particularly if the collecting is done extensively over a long period of time and is not merely a passing whim. It is interesting to note Darwin's remark that this tendency was "clearly innate." Also the kinds of things collected in childhood might give a clue as to ray type. While Darwin was studying to be a clergyman at Cambridge, his real interests clearly lay elsewhere: "No pursuit at Cambridge was followed with nearly so much eagerness or gave me so much pleasure as collecting beetles."[2]

"Verse-Making." As a school boy Darwin had difficulty writing poetry. "The school as a means of education to me was simply a blank. During my whole life I have been singularly incapable of mastering any language. Especial attention was paid to verse-making, and this I could never do well. I had many friends, and got together a grand collection of old verses, which by patching together, sometimes aided by other boys, I could work into any subject."[3]

"Verse-making" or writing poetry is something that the creatively and artistically inclined fourth ray mind generally finds much more appealing than the fifth ray mind. Webster defines poetry as "writing that formulates a concentrated imaginative awareness of experience in language chosen and arranged to create a specific emotional response through meaning, sound, and rhythm." Scientific minds are generally not concerned with an "imaginative awareness of experience" nor are they concerned with creating an "emotional response." It is more specifically the fourth ray type that employs the creative imagination to bring about an emotional response and to affect consciousness.

It is interesting to note the circuitous route the young Darwin settled upon in order to meet the academic requirements of "verse-making." Instead of using the imagination and exploring the subtleties of one's inner feelings and working creatively, he patched together fragments from a collection of old verses. It was as if he were endeavoring to solve a fourth ray problem with a fifth ray method. An exaggerated example of a similar situation in reverse is the well-known satire on the religious scholars who were endeavoring to discern the number of teeth in a horse's mouth by an intuitive method. When an apparently simple minded man suggested, "Why don't you *count* the teeth?" they brushed off the annoyance as if such a secular approach were beneath their dignity. The scholars in the exaggerated tale were endeavoring to use a fourth ray method to solve a problem readily accessible to a fifth ray method. The scholars were endeavoring to know intuitively when outer investigation would easily have sufficed. In order to create poetry, however, how equally absurd it is to take fragments of existing poems and rearrange them into a new piece. The assignment required an introspective approach; the young Darwin, however, turned it into an outer gathering, collecting, examining, arranging, much in the manner of a naturalist's field excursion.

Ability to Memorize. "Much attention," wrote Darwin of his school years, "was paid to learning by heart the lesson of the previous day; this I could effect with great facility learning forty of fifty lines of Virgil or Homer, whilst I was in morning chapel; but this exercise was utterly useless, for every verse was forgotten in forty-eight hours."[4] There may be a tendency for the fifth ray type of mind to have a greater facility in respect to learning by rote than the other two types. Memorization entails an emphasis on the outermost form aspect to the neglect of the content or meaning. A quick and facile familiarity with the form would tend to be a characteristic of the developed fifth ray mind. The fourth ray mind, it seems to me, would have the most difficulty in memorization, generally speaking. Without some recognition of meaning the form withers and dies, as evidenced by Darwin's forgetting of the verses within forty-eight hours. The ray of the physical body or brain might also be a factor in memorization. A fifth ray mind and seventh ray brain, hypothetically speaking, could possibly be especially conducive to a facile memory.

Careful, Minute, Accurate Observation. As a young school boy Darwin was already developing his powers of observation. "From reading White's *Selborne* I took pleasure in watching the habits of birds, and even made notes on the subject. In my simplicity I remember wondering why every gentleman did not become an ornithologist."[5] Taking note on the habits of birds would, indeed, be a strong indication of a budding fifth ray mind. Another catalyst in Darwin's scientific education was provided by his brother. "Towards the end of my school life, my brother worked hard at chemistry and made a fair laboratory with proper apparatus in the tool-house in the garden, and I was allowed to aid him as a servant in most of his experiments. He made all the gases and many compounds, and I read... several books on chemistry, such as Henry and Parkes' *Chemical Catechism*. The subject interested me greatly, and we often used to go on working till rather late at night. This was the best part of my education at school, for it showed me practically the meaning of experimental science."[6]

For the most part Darwin's scientific education occurred outside the academic setting through his own efforts. From the ages of twenty-two to twenty-seven he sailed on the H.M.S. *Beagle*, gathering extensive data that was to form the basis of his theory of evolution. "I have always felt that I owe to the voyage the first real training or education of my mind. I was led to attend closely to several branches of natural history, and thus my powers of observation were improved, though they were already fairly developed... During some part of the day I wrote my Journal, and took much pains in describing carefully and vividly all that I had seen; and this was a good practice."[7]

The training of his mind included as a primary factor the development of his powers of observation. Of a fellow scientist Darwin wrote that he was "chiefly remarkable for the minuteness of his observations and their perfect accuracy."[8] "As far as I can judge of myself I worked to the utmost during the voyage from the mere pleasure of investigation, and from my strong desire to add a few facts to the great mass of facts in natural sciences."[9] A "great mass of facts" constitutes a body of scientific knowledge or at least the foundation upon which a body of scientific knowledge rests.

A Fourth Ray Type Despising Science. This painstaking effort to refine the powers of observation and to add a few facts to an existing body of knowledge is an effort that is generally little understood or appreciated by the fourth ray type of mind. Of Thomas Caryle, Darwin wrote: "His mind seemed to me a very narrow one; even if all branches of science, which he despised, are excluded . . . he thought it a most ridiculous thing that anyone should care whether a glacier moved a little quicker or a little slower, or moved at all. As far as I could judge, I never met a man with a mind so ill-adapted for scientific research."[10] It is very likely that Carlyle had a fourth ray mind. (Carlyle is given as a first ray type in *Esoteric Psychology,* I, p. 202, which most likely refers to the soul ray.) Although Carlyle was a brilliant and influential person in his own field, his "mind was ill-adapted for scientific research." It was not so much a matter of intelligence in Carlyle's case as it was a matter of type. The fourth ray type of mind may have a tendency to think that patient observation and accumulation of data is either "a most ridiculous thing", a tedious thing, or a matter of little meaning or significance. This is particularly true when there is a pronounced two-four-six type.

Where did Carlyle's special abilities lie? According to Darwin: "No one can doubt about his extraordinary power of drawing vivid pictures of things and men—far more vivid, as it appears to me, than any drawn by Macaulay. Whether his pictures of men were true ones is another question . . . He has been all-powerful in impressing some grand moral truths on the minds of men."[11] Extraordinary power of drawing vivid word pictures suggests an ability to detect the dramatic element in events, which would include more than the bare physical facts, and it also suggests a certain imaginative and creative ability. Darwin questioned, however, the accuracy of these pictures. These factors of vivid word pictures, creativity, imagination, questionable accuracy and the impressing of grand moral truths are generally more indicative of the fourth ray type of mind than of the other types. It seems that the minds of these two prominent, gifted and developed men were not able to syncronize to a common vibration, figuratively speaking.

The Scientific and the Liberal Arts "Mental Set." This factor of different type and not different degrees of intelligence was noted by Gary Zukav in *The Dancing Wu Li Masters:*

Generally speaking, people can be grouped into two categories of intellectual preference. The first group prefers explorations which require a precision of logical processes. These are the people who become interested in the natural sciences and mathematics. They do not become scientists because of their education, they choose a scientific education because it gratifies their scientific mental set. The second group prefers explorations which involve the intellect in a less logically rigorous manner. These are the people who become interested in the liberal arts. They do not have a liberal arts mentality because of their education, they choose a liberal arts education because it gratifies their liberal arts mental set.[12]

Zukav was typifying somewhat the fourth and fifth ray "mental sets." Mathematics, however, does not come under the domain of the fifth ray exclusively. In the writings of D.K. we find mathematics associated with the third, fourth and fifth rays. The point that Zukav is making here is that there is a predisposition towards the logical, precision of science on the one hand and the less rigorously logical liberal arts explorations on the other hand, and, therefore, it is not so much a matter of education (environment) and conscious choice as one may be inclined to believe.

Clear and Cautious Conclusions. The type of older people one is attracted to as a youth often indicates one's own latent type. The young and impressionable Darwin made the following analysis of an older colleague: "His mind was characterized, as it appeared to me, by clearness, caution ,sound judgement and a good deal of originality. When I made any remark to him on Geology, he never rested until he saw the case clearly and often made me see it more clearly than I had done before. He would advance all possible objections to my suggestion, and even after these were exhausted would long remain dubious."[13] The developed fifth ray type is characterized by clearness, caution, dubiousness and exhaustive analysis. The sound judgement and originality might have been the result of other ray influences.

In a letter to L. Jenyns, Darwin wrote: "I have continued steadily reading and collecting facts on variation of domestic animals and plants, and on the question of what are species. I have a grand body of facts, and I think I can draw some conclusions . . . I shall not publish on this subject for several years." In another letter to the same person he wrote: "With respect to my far distant work on species, I must have expressed myself with singular inaccuracy if I led you to suppose that I meant to say that my conclusions are inevitable. They have become so after years of weighing puzzles, to myself *alone;* but in my wildest day-dream, I never expect more than to be able to show that there are two sides to the question of the immutability of species . . ."[14]

After long years of collecting "a grand body of facts", Darwin cautiously drew some conclusions, which merely showed that there were at least two sides to the question. Darwin presents a refined and very pronounced scientific type. It is possible that both the mind and the personality were on the fifth ray of concrete or scientific knowledge. A difference between the fifth and first ray mind is that the fifth ray type tends to see fact leading to knowledge and knowledge as being an end in itself. The first ray type tends to see fact and knowledge as a means to some other end. The first ray type tends to be quick to take knowledge and apply it to social action, service, business or some institutionalized activity. As a result of these tendencies, the knowledge of the scientific type tends to be more comprehensive, more thorough, whereas the knowledge of the first ray type may be lacking in terms of a "grand body of facts" but may be greater in terms of applicability or "skill-in-action." It may be helpful to repeat this important distinction from time to time, looking at it from slightly different angles.

Darwin and Thoreau Contrasted. The following is a paragraph taken at random from Darwin's *Journal of Researches* written during the voyage of the H.M.S. *Beagle:*

> October 1st, 1833. We started by moonlight and arrived at the Rio Tercero by sunrise. This river is also called the Saladillo, and it deserves the name for the water is brackish. I stayed here the greater part of the day, searching for fossil bones. Besides a perfect tooth of the Toxodon, and many scattered bones, I found two immense skeletons near each other, projecting in bold relief from the perpendicular cliff of the Parana. They were, however, so completely decayed, that I could only bring away small fragments of one of the great molar teeth; but these are sufficient to show that the remains belonged to a Mastodon, probably to the same species with that, which formerly must have inhabited the Cordillera in Upper Peru in such great numbers. The men who took me in the canoe, said they had long known of these skeletons, and had often wondered how they had got there: the necessity of a theory being

felt, they came to the conclusion that, like the bizcacha, the mastodon was formerly a burrowing animal! In the evening we rode another stage, and crossed the Monge, another brackish stream, bearing the dregs of the washings of the Pampas.[15]

Darwin was twenty-four at the time of that notation. In 1839 (six years after Darwin had written the above entry) Thoreau went on a river voyage, later described in his first book *A Week on the Concord and Merrimack Rivers*.

Whether we live by the sea-side, or by the lakes and rivers, or on the prairie, it concerns us to attend to the nature of fishes, since they are not phenomena confined to certain localities only, but forms and phases of the life in nature universally dispersed. The countless shoals which annually coast the shores of Europe and America are not so interesting to the student of nature as the more fertile law itself, which deposits their spawn on the tops of mountains, and on the interior plains; the fish principle in nature, from which it results that they may be found in water in so many places, in greater or less numbers. The natural historian is not a fisherman, who prays for cloudy days and good luck merely, but as fishing has been styled "a contemplative man's recreation," introducing him profitably to woods and water, so the fruit of the naturalist's observation is not in new genera or species, but in new contemplations still, and science is only a more contemplative man's recreation. The seeds of the life of fishes are everywhere disseminated, whether the winds waft them, or the waters float them, or the deep earth holds them; wherever a pond is dug, straightway it is stocked with this vivacious race. They have a lease of nature, and it is not yet out. The Chinese are bribed to carry their ova from province to province in jars or in hollow reeds, or the water-birds to transport them to the mountain tarns and interior lakes. There are fishes wherever there is a fluid medium, and even in clouds and in melted metals we detect their semblance. Think how in winter you can sink a line down straight in a pasture through snow and through ice, and pull up a bright, slippery, dumb, subterranean silver or golden fish! It is curious, also, to reflect how they make one family, from the largest to the smallest. The least minnow, that lies on the ice as bait for pickerel, looks like a huge seafish cast up on the shore. In the waters of this town there are about a dozen distinct species, though the inexperienced would expect many more.[16]

In Darwin's paragraph once again we see the scientific qualities of clarity, of concern with fact, of one little observation to be added to a grand body of fact, and of cautious, tentative conclusion. Thoreau's paragraph is ambiguous and confusing. It has to be read at least twice to discern basically what he was talking about. Thoreau came to regard himself not as a naturalist but as a natural philosopher (as shall be brought out in the chapter on Thoreau), but the distinction was apparently not clear to him at the time of his early writings. The paragraph is closer to a celebration of fishes than it is to a naturalist's observation of fact. In the first sentence Thoreau stated that we ought to attend to the nature of fishes because they are universally dispersed. Does this mean that if something is not "universally dispersed", if something is a very rare phenomenon, that we ought not to concern ourselves with it? The second sentence is a confusing one, indeed: "Countless shoals", that is, schools of fish along the "shores of Europe and America are not so interesting . . . as the more fertile law" which seems to be the "fish principle in nature." In other words, it is more interesting to consider how fish eggs are carried to remote inland lakes than it is to consider the schools of salt-water fish, which propagate, shall we say then, under a less fertile law? The following sentence is perhaps the most senseless one from a scientific or fifth ray point of view: "There are fishes wherever there is fluid medium, and even in clouds and in melted metals we detect their semblance." The first statement is inaccurate and the second is irrelevant to the matter under discussion.

Although the above paragraph from Thoreau is probably one of his worst, nevertheless it is interesting to note that, similar to Darwin's characterization of Carlyle, Thoreau had an "extraordinary power of drawing vivid pictures of things and men", (word pictures that may not always have been accurate), and he was making an effort to impress "some grand moral truths on the minds of men." Thoreau was not observing in the detached manner of the fifth ray scientific mind, he was making moral or value judgements in that he was frequently, almost continually, saying that something is *better* than something else, that this is what *should* concern us, that this is the direction we *ought* to go, etc. His main message in the above paragraph is that we ought to contemplate the wonders of nature, for mysteries of Diety are concealed therein. It is a mystic rather than a strictly scientific experience, as shall be shown in subsequent quotes. It is important to realize, however, that these divergent attitudes can be blended in one person to the benefit of the work at hand, in whatever field it may be.

If we compare Darwin and Thoreau not in a scientific situation but in an artistic one, that is, one that requires a certain sensitivity to beauty rather than detached observation of fact, then the picture becomes a different one. Darwin made the following statement in the last few pages of his *Journal:*

> The pleasure derived from beholding the scenery and the general aspect of the various countries we have visited, has decidedly been the most constant and highest source of enjoyment. It is probable that the picturesque beauty of many parts of Europe exceeds anything which we beheld. But there is a growing pleasure in comparing the character of the scenery in different countries, which to a certain degree is distinct from merely admiring its beauty. It depends chiefly on an acquaintance with the individual parts of each view: I am strongly induced to believe that as in music, the person who understands every note will, if he also possesses a proper taste, more thoroughly enjoy the whole, so he who examines each part of a fine view, may also thoroughly comprehend the full and combined effect. Hence, a traveller should be a botanist, for in all views plants form the chief embellishment.[17]

On the one hand we have an admiration of beauty, an enjoyment and a derived pleasure, while on the other hand we have a "comparing the character" of different scenery, "examining each part of a fine view." Admiration-enjoyment is more of an emotional experience, while comparing-examining is more of an intellectual experience. If these two experiences can be seen as a polarity, Darwin clearly favored the comparing-examining side. In fact, his admiration-enjoyment depended largely on how much he knew or had analyzed. To admire more, one had to know more, so that is the direction he pursued.

Considering Thoreau, however, one would have to say that he admired more than he knew concretely and clearly. Admiration at a relatively unrefined level could be equated with pleasure and enjoyment, which are the words Darwin used. But admiration carried to a finer degree becomes appreciation and love. Love enables one to see, that is to discover the meaning and to understand, also to identify the quality of the life veiled by the form. Other words typifying the finer experience are wonder, awe, a sense of beauty and unity.

Compare Thoreau's account to the foregoing one of Darwin:

> Then, when supper was done, and we had written the journal of our voyage, we wrapped our buffaloes about us, and lay down with our heads pillowed on our arms, listening awhile to the distant baying of a dog, or the murmurs of the river, or to the wind, which had not gone to rest . . . or half awake and half asleep, dreaming of a star which glimmered through our cotton roof. Perhaps at midnight one was awakened by a cricket shrilly singing on his shoulder, or by a hunting spider in his eye, and was lulled asleep again by some streamlet purling its way along at the bottom of a wooded and rocky ravine in our neighborhood. It was pleasant to lie with our heads so low in the grass, and hear what a tinkling ever-busy laboratory it was. A thousand little artisans beat on their anvils all night long . . .
>
> There is no doubt that the loftiest written wisdom is either rhymed, or in some way musically measured,—is, in form as well as substance, poetry; and a volume which should contain the condensed wisdom of mankind, need not have one rhythmless line.
>
> Yet poetry, though the last and finest result, is a natural fruit. As naturally as the oak bears an acorn, and the vine a gourd, man bears a poem, either spoken or done. It is the chief and most memorable success, for history is but a prose narrative of poetic deeds.[18]

Darwin thought that the traveler ought to be a botanist, for to become acquainted with the individual parts helps in admiring the view and "plants form the chief embellishment" in any view. Thoreau thought, apparently, that the traveler ought to be a poet. None of the "individual parts" does he examine very closely—the cricket, the spider, the streamlet, etc.—nor does he feel any special need to examine them closely. Yet his admiration, joy and awe of nature is profound. He endeavored to live a poem as well as write one, and Nature was his great teacher. He went so far as to say that "It is the worshippers of beauty, after all, who have done the real pioneer work of the world."[19] Both Darwin and Thoreau were developed and pronounced ray types. They took excursions into and looked out over the natural environment and saw entirely different things. While Darwin admired and enjoyed the picturesque beauty of the scenery, Thoreau worshipped it. While Darwin patiently accumulated a grand mass of facts in order to further knowledge, Thoreau referred to such things as "bald natural facts" and made no effort to contribute to that type of knowledge.

Atrophying of the Higher Aesthetic Tastes. Darwin's intensive, specialized scientific labors bore their fruits but also took their toll. In the following passage Darwin made some interesting observations of his own psychological processes.

> This curious and lamentable loss of the higher aesthetic tastes is all the odder, as books on history, biographies and travels (independently of any scientific facts which they may contain), and essays on all sorts of subjects interest me as much as ever they did. My mind seems to have become a kind of machine for grinding general laws out of large collections of facts, but why this should have caused the atrophy of that part of the brain alone, on which the higher tastes depend, I cannot conceive. A man with a mind more highly organized or better constituted than mine, would not I suppose have thus suffered; and if I had to live my life again I would have made a rule to read some poetry and listen to some music at least once every week; for perhaps the parts of my brain now atrophied could thus have been kept active through use. The loss of these tastes is a loss of happiness, and may possibly be injurious to the intellect, and more probably to the moral character, by enfeebling the emotional part of our nature.[20]

Darwin felt a definite lack in the following areas: "higher aesthetic tastes", poetry, music, "moral character", "the emotional part of our nature", and he felt an unhappiness that stems from a feeling of incompleteness or lack of wholeness. Van Gogh, as we have seen, was terribly out of balance along that line of aesthetic tastes and emotional sensitivity and, although achieving specialized excellence, could well have used such fifth ray qualities as clarity of thought, reason, detachment, analysis and careful observation. Gandhi was well-balanced along both of these two major lines (2-4-6 and 1-3-5-7) and participated intelligently in the three types of energies under discussion (1-4-5).

It is questionable whether "reading some poetry and listening to some music at least once every week" would be sufficient to prevent the "atrophy of that part of the brain on which the higher tastes depend." Reading and listening are generally passive and, therefore, not as effective in developing capacity to attune to and manipulate certain energies as more active processes would be, such as composing music and writing poetry. Similarly, listening to a scientific lecture once a week would generally not be sufficient to develop the scientific attitude, whereas undertaking a scientific project involving experimentation, minute observation, etc., would provide a much better opportunity for activating latent energies.

Francis Darwin wrote of his father Charles: "His literary tastes and opinions were not on a level with the rest of his mind. He himself, though he was clear as to what he thought good, considered that in matters of literary tastes he was quite outside the pale, and often spoke of what those within it liked or disliked, as if they formed a class to which he had no claim to belong."[21]

A Troublesome Correspondent. Darwin made it a point to answer all letters sent to him. According to his son Francis:

> He had a printed form to be used in replying to troublesome correspondents, but he hardly ever used it; I suppose he never found an occasion on which it might have been used with advantage. He received a letter from a stranger stating that the writer had undertaken to uphold Evolution at a debating society, and that being a busy young man, without time for reading, he wished to have a sketch of my father's views. Even this wonderful man got a civil answer, though I think he did not get much material for his speech.[22]

Apparently this young man, who had little time for reading but who nevertheless wanted to participate in a formal debate in defense of evolution, was the worst or one of the worst correspondents with whom Darwin had to deal. From a scientific point of view we can understand why Darwin almost resorted to sending a form letter. The fifth ray mind would not enter a debate without having thorough knowledge of the subject—knowledge being always the main factor. From a first ray point of view, however, this is not necessarily the case, and it is my guess that the young man (who was too busy, or too active to read) had a first ray mind. Skill in debating can be demonstrated in such a way that one can debate either side to a question, personal opinion or knowledge being far secondary factors. Also people with much knowledge may not be skillful debaters. The knowledgable person will want to go into great detail and lengthy explanation. The debater will affirm significant points, making no attempt to go into a formal proof. The first ray type also likes to have lines of communication open to the sources of knowledge but may not have that kind of detailed knowledge oneself. Thus, the young man wishing to debate evolution saw nothing wrong in trying to procure an outline from Darwin, nor in debating with inadequate knowledge from the scientific point of view.

Reason at the Summit of the Faculties of the Human Mind. In *Descent of Man* Darwin discussed whether or not certain faculties present in man are also present in animals. Among these are imagination and reason.

> The Imagination is one of the highest prerogatives of man. By this faculty he unites former images and ideas, independently of the will, and thus creates brilliant and novel results ... The value of the products of our imagination depends of course on the number, accuracy, and clearness of our impressions, on our judgement and taste in selecting or rejecting the involuntary combinations, and to a certain extent on our power of voluntarily combining them....
>
> Of all the faculties of the human mind, it will, I presume, be admitted that Reason stands at the summit.[23]

Darwin placed reason higher than the imagination and at the summit of "all the faculties of the human mind," which the fifth ray type of mind would generally tend to do. According to Darwin the imagination "unites former images and ideas", which is to say that much in the manner of Darwin's earlier "verse-making" the imagination gathers a fragment here, a scrap there, and patches the various pieces together. The imagination is a creative process. Darwin, however, tried to circumvent the creative process by selecting and juxtaposing pieces that had already been created. He recognized the value of the imagination but was not a very imaginative person himself and, therefore, had trouble with its definition. His statement that the "value of the products of our imagination depends on the number, accuracy, and clearness of our impressions" suggests that he was talking more about the process of reasoning than about the imagination. For example, if we make a couple of substitutions: "the value of the products of our *reasonings* depends on the number, accuracy, and clearness of our *observations*," the sentence would make much more sense.

Moral Faculties and Intellectual Powers. Also in *Descent of Man* Darwin discussed the moral factor in man and animals.

> The moral faculties are generally and justly esteemed as of higher value than the intellectual powers. But we should bear in mind that the activity of the mind in vividly recalling past impressions is one of the fundamental though secondary bases of conscience. This affords the strongest argument for educating and stimulating in all possible ways the intellectual faculties of every human being. No doubt a man with a torpid mind, if his social affections and sympathies are well developed, will be led to good actions, and may have a fairly sensitive conscience. But whatever renders the imagination more vivid and strengthens the habit of recalling and comparing past impressions, will make the conscience more sensitive, and may even somewhat compensate for weak social affections and sympathies.
>
> The moral nature of man has reached its present standard, partly through the advancement of his reasoning powers and consequently of a just public opinion, but especially from his sympathies having been rendered more tender and widely diffused through the effects of habit, example, instruction, and reflection.[24]

In his first statement that the moral faculties are generally esteemed higher than intellectual powers, it may be noted that Darwin was not trying to impress upon the reader some "grand moral truths" in the manner of Carlyle or Thoreau, he was merely making an observation in regard to public opinion. Even though, according to Darwin, the moral nature or conscience is not strictly dependent upon reasoning powers, nevertheless the intellectual and reasoning powers do play an important "secondary" role. "Recalling and comparing" are the words he used to describe this contributing role. "Vividly recalling past impressions" provides the data, the points of observations, the facts with which one can work. "Comparing past impressions" is the reasoning about the facts. If these are secondary factors, it seems that the primary factors are "habit, example, instruction and reflection." "Habit", then according to Darwin, is the source or the first appearance of the moral nature. Habit, we can surmise from Darwin's thought, came about by chance: a primitive person came upon a mode of conduct quite by chance, formed a habit, and his habit provided an "example" to others, which was eventually encoded in a body of "instruction," which in turn was fortified by intellectual "reflection." Neither a chance act which eventually solidifies into a habit nor reasoning powers are the primary moral developers. Historically, religion has played the role of primary moral developer. Religion, however, deals with such things as non-physical or invisible and superhuman sources, ritual, inspiration, intuition, spiritual authority, knowing through love and devotion, the archetypal ideal, etc.— all of which can be unpalatable to the strict and pronounced scientific thinker, particularly during the stages of intellectual and personality development when religion, philosophy and science can be temporarily separated. Since it is difficult to objectify the subjective and to get a scientific grip on relatively abstract factors, the fifth ray mind may have a tendency to negate or avoid them. Darwin discerned well the contributing factor of reason, the faculty of mind which the scientific type tends to refine so well. But in respect to such matters as imagination, morality, beauty, religion, etc., his discussion was peripheral.

It is interesting to note that, according to Darwin, reason will help "compensate for weak social affections and sympathies." If Darwin had had to choose between morality-conscience-sympathies on the one hand and intellect-reason on the other, it is likely he would have chosen reason, for reason was most highly prized and through reason, he believed, one could arrive at morality. Thoreau, on the other hand, wrote: "Ignorance and bungling with love are better than wisdom and skill without."[25] If we substitute the word "intellect" or "reason" for the word "wisdom", since, strictly speaking, wisdom is never devoid of love, then Thoreau's meaning becomes clearer: Ignorance and bungling with love are better than reason and skill without. If Thoreau had had to choose between conscience-morality-love on the one hand and intellect-reason on the other, he would obviously have chosen love. When we have a pronouced fifth ray type, as in Darwin's case, and a fourth ray mind with a strong second ray influence, as in Thoreau's case, this demarcation between intellect-reason and morality-love may be starkly evident.

In discussing religion, Darwin wrote: "The same high mental faculties which first led man to believe in unseen spiritual agencies, then in fetishism, polytheism, and ultimately in monotheism, would infallibly lead him, as long as his reasoning powers remained poorly developed, to various strange superstitions and customs. Many of these are terrible to think of—such as the sacrifice of human beings to a blood-loving god; with trial of innocent persons by the ordeal of poison or fire; witchcraft, etc.—yet it is well occasionally to reflect on these superstitions, for they show us what an infinite debt of gratitude we owe to the improvement of our reason, to science, and to our accumulated knowledge."[26] Emotional development without reason provides a fertile ground for superstition. A major contribution of the fifth ray is the application of clear reason to all fields of endeavor, religion included. The fact that reason can also run astray suggests merely that it, too, is not complete unto itself but a needed part within a larger whole.

Contrast with the Fourth Ray "Poetic Faculties." Looking through Thoreau's writings for a comment on reason, I can find none. "I found in myself," wrote Thoreau, "and still find, an instinct toward a higher, or, as it is named, spiritual life, as do most men, and another toward a primitive rank and savage one, and I reverence them both."[27] The man conditioned by the fourth ray of harmony through conflict may experience an interplay of conflicting opposites more dramatically than others. The factor of "instinct" here is a non-rational one that functions on both a higher and a lower level. That is, the lower instinct is clearly a non-rational factor, for it is present in non-rational beings. But there is also, according to Thoreau, a higher instinct that guides one in the spiritual life, which suggests a super-rational factor. Unlike Darwin, apparently, Thoreau did not place reason at the summit of the mental life. In the statement: "I believe that every man who has ever been earnest to preserve his higher or poetic faculties in the best condition has been particularly inclined to abstain from animal food, and from much food of any kind"—we find the faculty of mind that Thoreau prized most highly, the "higher or poetic faculties."

If one listens to the faintest but constant suggestions of his genius, which are certainly true, he sees not to what extremes, or even insanity, it may lead him; and yet that way, as he grows more resolute and faithful, his roads lies. The faintest assured objection which one healthy man feels will at length prevail over the arguments and customs of mankind. No man ever followed his genius till it misled him. Though the result were bodily weakness, yet perhaps no one can say that the consequences were to be regretted, for these were a life in conformity to high principles. If the day and the night are such that you greet them with joy, and life emits a fragrance like flowers and sweet-scented herbs, is more elastic, more starry, more immortal,—that is your success . . . The greatest gains and values are farthest from being appreciated. We easily come to doubt if they exist. We soon forget them. They are the highest reality. Perhaps the facts most astounding and most real are never communicated by man to man. The true harvest of my daily life is somewhat as intangible and indescribable as the tints of morning or evening. It is a little star-dust caught, a segment of the rainbow which I have clutched."[28]

On his scale of important faculties Thoreau gave special prominence to: a higher and lower instinct, "poetic faculties", genius, and a sense of joy. Also important are the "spiritual life", "higher principles" and the ill-appreciated and very elusive "highest reality." In contrast to the first ray emphasis on the act, the deed, the skill-in-action, practical responsibility, power, and in contrast to the fifth ray emphasis on clear reason and the observable, provable fact, Thoreau emphasized the indescribable, intangible, non-communicable, elusive factors that he poetically likened to the fragrance of flowers and the tints of a sunrise. In contrast to the first and fifth ray types, the fourth ray type tends to be least in touch with the dense physical plane.

"Classical and Romantic." Other writers and observers have remarked on differences in type or "mental set" or temperament. Robert Pirsig in his book *Zen and the Art of Motorcycle Maintenance* characterized "two realities, one of immediate artistic appearance and one of underlying scientific explanation, and they don't match and they don't fit and they really don't have much of anything to do with one another."[29] He typifies these two realities as "classical understanding and romantic understanding. . . . A classical understanding sees the world primarily as underlying form itself. A romantic understanding sees it primarily in terms of immediate appearance." Romantic understanding "is primarily inspirational, imaginative, creative, intuitive. Feeling rather than facts predominate. 'Art' when it is opposed to 'Science' is often romantic. It does not proceed by reason or by laws. It proceeds by feelings, intuition and esthetic conscience.... The classic style is straightforward, unadorned, unemotional, economical and carefully proportioned. Its purpose is not to inspire emotionally, but to bring order out of chaos and to make the unknown known.[30]

Clearly, Pirsig was differentiating between the fourth and fifth ray mental type. "Art," he noted, "when it is opposed to science is often romantic." When the artistic type is opposed to science, the presence of the fourth ray is likely. All art is not opposed to science, as Pirsig implied. "Inspirational, imaginative, esthetic conscience, creative, intuitive, feeling" are words that approximate the fourth ray type—"immediate appearance" far less so. "Straightforward" (clear), "unadorned" (precise and to the point), "unemotional" (rational), "economical", "making the unknown known" all typify the "classical" or scientific type.

> To a romantic this classic mode often appears dull, awkward and ugly, like mechanical maintenance itself. Everything is in terms of pieces and parts and components and relationships. Nothing is figured out until it's run through the computer a dozen times. Everything's got to be measured and proved. Oppressive. Heavy. Endlessly grey. The death force.
>
> Within the classic mode, however, the romantic has some appearances of his own. Frivolous, irrational, erratic, untrustworthy, interested primarily in pleasure-seeking. Shallow. Of no substance. Often a parasite who cannot or will not carry his own weight. A real drag on society. By now these battle lines should sound a little familiar.[31]

Excessive analysis and classification of the form can seem "oppressive" to the fourth ray type. The negative side or distortion of this energy can lead the fifth ray type into minute analysis of trivial and insignificant matters. The quest of the fourth ray type toward beauty, harmony and transcendental understanding can appear to be of little substance and little rationality to the fifth ray type. A negative side of this energy can lead the fourth ray type into "pleasure-seeking" or into an attempt at transcendence that never gets above the enjoyment of the astral-emotional plane. The result is being a prisoner of one's moods and desires.

There is, however, a strong tendency to recognize the hidden value of types like our own and to see the surface flaws of types unlike our own. As Pirsig mentioned:

> Persons tend to think and feel exclusively in one mode or the other and in doing so tend to misunderstand and underestimate what the other mode is all about. But no one is willing to give up the truth as he sees it, and as far as I know, no one now living has any real reconciliation of these truths of modes. There is no point at which these visions of reality are unified.
>
> And so in recent times we have seen a huge split develop between a classic culture and a romantic counterculture—two worlds growing alienated and hateful toward each other with everyone wondering if it will always be this way, a house divided against itself. No one wants it really—despite what his antagonists in the other dimension might think.[32]

In the effort to reconcile the two modes of approach Pirsig mentioned that "about the Buddha that exists independently of analytic thought much has been said.... But about the Buddha that exists *within* analytic thought, and *gives that analytic thought its direction,* virtually nothing has been said..."[33] The mystic approach tends to see the Godhead or Truth in terms of an intuitively experienced Oneness or transcendent state that defies analysis and that can only become something less through analysis. On the other hand, the analytic thought (one of the means of "inducing soul control"[34]) that differentiates and divides is a key factor in the process of knowing and the nature of knowledge. Van Gogh emphasized knowing through the heart, through love, through a feeling of oneness. The scientific mind emphasizes knowing through a thorough analysis of the form, the part—its laws and relationships. Pirsig discovered, preceeding from the scientific approach, how both are essential.

The same thought of reconciling these two modes of approach is a major theme of Fritjof Capra's *Tao of Physics:* "Throughout history, it has been recognized that the human mind is capable of two kinds of knowledge, or two modes of consciousness, which has been associated with science and religion, respectively. In the West, the intuitive, religious type of knowledge is often devalued in favor of rational, scientific knowledge, whereas the traditional Eastern attitude is in general just the opposite."[35] "Rational knowledge is derived from the experience we have with objects and events in our everyday environment. It belongs to the realm of the intellect, whose function is to discriminate, divide, compare, measure and categorize."[36] Mystic knowledge Capra characterized as "the direct experience of undifferentiated, undivided, indeterminate 'suchness.' Complete apprehension of this suchness is not only the core of Eastern mysticism, but is the central characteristic of all mystical experience."[37]

This does not mean, however, that the scientific type cannot tap intuitive levels. Neither does it mean that all fourth ray minds are mystical, religious and intuitive. Some first and fifth ray types can be far more religious than some fourth ray types. Capra pointed out that "the rational part of research would, in fact, be useless if it were not complemented by the intuition that gives scientists new insights and makes them creative."[38] In other words, scientific researach at an advanced level requires as a complement the mystical mode of thought as well. At less advanced stages a strictly rational endeavor would tend to suffice. Similarly with the other types of mind. To put it another way: at certain levels of consciousness we can divide intellectual endeavors into such areas as religion, science and philosophy, and we can pursue knowledge within the self-imposed limitations of these categories. At a more refined level of consciousness, however, it becomes impossible to proceed without including all three of these modes of inquiry.

Observing, Collecting, Explaining. In a letter to Dr. Abbott, Darwin wrote: "At no time am I a quick thinker or writer: whatever I have done in science has solely been by long pondering, patience and industry." Summing up his qualities in his autobiography he wrote:

> My power to follow a long and purely abstract train of thought is very limited; I should, moreover, never have succeeded with metaphysics or mathematics. My memory is extensive, yet hazy. ... So poor in one sense is my memory, that I have never been able to remember for more than a few days a single date or line of poetry. ...

73

On the favourable side of the balance, I think that I am superior to the common run of men in noticing things which easily escape attention, and in observing them carefully. My industry has been nearly as great as it could have been in the observation and collection of facts.... From my early youth I have had the strongest desire to understand or explain whatever I observe,— that is, to group all facts under some general laws. These causes combined have given me the patience to reflect or ponder for any number of years over any unexplained problems.[39]

Summary. The habit of collecting all sorts of things in childhood may indicate the presence of the fifth ray. The fifth ray type of mind may tend to have an aversion to the creative process of writing poetry. There may be a tendency for the fifth ray type of mind to have a greater facility in learning through memorization than the other two types. Darwin as a school boy not only "took pleasure in watching the habits of birds" but "even took notes on the subject." This was a self-initiated effort. "Minuteness of observations and their perfect accuracy" were qualities admired by the young Darwin. The fourth ray type of mind may have a tendency to think that patient observation and accumulation of data is either "a most ridiculous thing," a tedious thing, or a matter of little meaning or significance.

Zukav typified two kinds of "mental sets" as the "scientific" and the "liberal arts." The scientific mental set deals with "precision of logical processes," while the liberal arts mental set involves the intellect in a "less logically rigorous manner." The developed fifth ray mind is characterized by clearness, caution, dubiousness, and exhaustive analysis. In contrast to the fifth ray mind's tendency to observe fact and determine cause and effect relationships, the fourth ray mind may have a tendency to impress some grand moral truths on the minds of men. While Darwin "derived pleasure from beholding the scenery," Thoreau was a "worshipper of beauty."

Darwin lamented his "loss of the higher aesthetic tastes." He felt a lack in terms of poetry, music, moral character and the emotional part of his nature. The fifth ray mind would not enter a debate without having a thorough knowledge of the subject matter. A person with much knowledge might not necessarily be a skillful debater, for there may be the tendency to go into lengthy and tedious detail. Of all the faculties of the human mind, Darwin considered reason to stand at the summit. He thought that the advancement of reason had much to do with the advancement of the moral nature of man. Reason could help compensate for the lack of social affections and sympathies. According to Darwin, we owe an "infinite debt of gratitude to the improvement of our reason, to science, and to our accumulated knowledge," for they have done much to eradicate the evils of superstition. Thoreau placed the "poetic faculties", genius and a sense of joy higher than the intellectual reasoning faculties.

Robert Pirsig characterized "two realities" as the "classical" and the "romantic." The "classical" would correspond to the scientific: straightforward, unadorned, unemotional, economical, making the unknown known. The "romantic" would correspond to the fourth ray type: inspirational, imaginative, aesthetic conscience, creative, intuitive, feeling. "Persons tend to think and feel exclusively in one mode or the other and in doing so tend to misunderstand and underestimate what the other mode is all about." Fritjof Capra characterized two kinds of knowledge. The function of one kind is to "discriminate, divide, compare, measure, and categorize," which would correspond to the fifth ray type. The other he characterized as a mystic type of knowledge, which deals with a "direct experience of undifferentiated, undivided, indeterminate suchness." This is more suggestive of the fourth ray type.

Darwin had difficulty with a purely abstract train of thought. He felt that his superior attributes were in "noticing things which easily escape attention and in observing them carefully." There was the "strongest desire to understand or explain whatever I observed."

REFERENCE NOTES TO CHAPTER IV

1. Charles Darwin, *Autobiography* (New York: W. W. Norton and Company, 1969), p. 23.
2. Ibid., p. 62.
3. Ibid., pp. 27-28.
4. Ibid., p. 28.
5. Ibid., p. 44.
6. Ibid., p. 17.
7. Ibid., pp. 78, 79.
8. Ibid., p. 103.
9. Ibid., p. 81.
10. Ibid., pp. 113-14.
11. Ibid., pp. 113-14.
12. Gary Zukav, *The Dancing Wu Li Masters* (New York: William Morrow and Company, Inc., 1979), p. 23.
13. Darwin, *Autobiography*, p. 100.
14 Charles Darwin, *Selected Letters*, ed. Francis Darwin (New York: Dover Publications, Inc., 1958, first published D. Appleton & Co., 1892).
15. Charles Darwin, *Journal of Researches into the Natural History and Geology of the Countries visited during the voyage of the H.M.S. Beagle round the world under the command of Captain Fitz Roy* (London: John Murray, Albemarle Street, 1907).
16. Henry David thoreau, *A Week on the Concord and Merrimack Rivers* (self-published, 1849).
17. Darwin, *Journal*, pp. 502-3.
18. Thoreau, *Concord and Merrimack*.
19. Ibid.
20. Darwin, *Autobiography*, p. 139.
21. Darwin, *Selected Letters*, p. 83.
22. Ibid., p. 79.
23. Darwin, *Descent of Man* (first published 1871), Chapter III.
24. Ibid., Chapter XXI.
25. Thoreau, *Concord and Merrimack*.
26. Darwin, *Descent of Man*, Chapter III.
27. Thoreau, *Walden*, "Higher Laws".
28. Ibid.
29. Robert Pirsig, *Zen and the Art of Motorcycle Maintenance* (New York: Bantam Books, Inc., 1975), p. 54.
30. Ibid., pp. 66, 67.
31. Ibid., p. 67.
32. Ibid., pp. 67-68.
33. Ibid., p. 77.
34. Bailey, *Esoteric Psycholocy*, II, pp. 250-4.

35. Fritjof Capra, *The Tao of Physics* (New York: Bantam Books, Inc., 1977, first published Boulder, Colorado: Shambhala Publications, 1976), p. 14.

36. Ibid., p. 14.

37. Ibid., p. 16.

38. Ibid., p. 18.

39. Darwin, *Autobiography,* p. 140.

Chapter V

Mahatma Gandhi: First Ray Mind

Mohanda Karamchand Gandhi, known as the "Mahatma" or Great Soul, was born in Porbandar India in 1869. He studied law in London, then moved to South Africa where he worked as a lawyer and fought for the civil rights of the Indian immigrants. There he evolved a non-violent method of social protest that he later used so successfully in India. On his return to India in 1914 he fought for Indian independence from Britain, which finally came about in 1947.

The Importance of Facts. When Gandhi was working on a legal case in South Africa, an associate of his said to him: " 'Gandhi, I have learnt one thing, and it is this, that if we take care of the facts of a case, the law will take care of itself. Let us dive deeper into the facts of this case.' With these words he asked me to study the case further and then see him again. . . .

"When I was making preparation for Dada Abdulla's case, I had not fully realized the paramount importance of facts. Facts mean truth, and once we adhere to truth, the law comes to our aid naturally."[1]

The attitude of mind that realizes the "paramount importance of facts" in this sense suggests the possibility of a first ray mind. As the first ray turns its attention to "things concrete", to "governing" and to administrative type work, it must necessarily be concerned with what has been called "fact." Facts are also of foundational importance to the fifth ray mind, but it is a different order of facts that interests the scientific type. Facts tend not to hold the same "paramount importance" to the fourth ray mental type as they do for the other two types. According to Thoreau, "the lawyer's truth is not Truth, but consistency or a consistent expediency. Truth is always in harmony with herself, and is not concerned chiefly to reveal the justice that may consist with wrong-doing."[2] Gandhi's "facts mean truth" and

Thoreau's "the lawyer's truth is not Truth" appear contradictory, but both are true from the relative perspective of the different ray types. Gandhi's truth is a concrete matter. Thoreau was more concerned with philosophical Truth or perhaps with an Absolute Truth that "is always in harmony with herself." Instead of the truth of a particular incident, Thoreau (with his strong second and fourth ray note) was concerned with Truth for all time. One approach is more vital and immediate, the other approach tends to be more speculative and future oriented.

In respect to the importance of facts, the fourth ray mind is most unlike the other two types, which results in many clashes and misunderstandings of a characteristic nature. Consider the following occurrence reported in a book entitled *All You Know is Facts.*

> Some time more than twenty years ago, on a spring afternoon in Cambridge Common, a young lady and I were passing time in that humid haze of tenderness and self-importance which is the atmosphere of a student love affair. I recall, uncertainly, that we were talking about poetry. This was a subject she was "studying" and I was not, but W.H. Auden had come to town not long before to give a reading, and I had done a piece about him for the wartime version of the Harvard *Crimson.* As I reconstruct the conversation, my lady made some references to a poem of Auden's, and I told her when and where it was first published and what collection it was in and probably something about alterations between first publication and first collected editions. As I was drawing breath to continue her enlightenment, she rose to her feet in uncontrollable annoyance and said in the most cutting voice she could command, "You! All *you* know is facts."[3]

On the one hand, we have a person who is involved in the field of journalism—a field that is concerned with the reporting of significant facts and not with a creative type of writing nor with philosophical interpretation—a person who prides himself on knowing certain particulars about publication dates, alterations, collected editions, etc. On the other hand, we have a person who is thoroughly annoyed with this *type of knowledge* and who is studying poetry undoubtedly from an altogether different point of view.

The author of *All You Know is Facts* went on to say:

Well, I can tell you, I was upset; and for a long time, too. Today, though, if the "bad" word *facts* can be changed to the "good" word *information,* I will own the criticism calmly. I believe in information. Often, when I am boring all around me by putting together *viva voce* the pieces of some puzzle I am about to describe in print, people will ask for my opinion on some part of the story, whether I think it is a good or a bad thing, and I have a terrible trouble answering them. I cannot even be trusted to give a simple answer to the reasonable and despairing question about what some piece of data *means,* because I can usually see 'and rarely refrain from explaining' several possible meanings, none of which should be ignored. My job as I understand it is to get the picture right; and if you get the picture right people select from your prose partial and directed perceptions similar to those they select from reality; and that's fine.[4]

Once again we see certain polarities occurring that help to reveal ray type: fact, information, accuracy, letting the facts speak for themselves on the one hand, and a concern with opinion, meaning, the moral or value or "good" or "bad" of an issue on the other. The writer-journalist is clearly puzzled by the point of view that is more concerned with meaning-interpretation than with fact-information. Others are bored with fact and want to discuss the values involved. We find the first ray and the fourth ray type of mind in conflict here. The admonishment "all you know is facts" upset him deeply, because something close to the very heart of his mode of thinking was under attack. Over the years nothing seemed to have really changed: He simply substituted the word "information" for "facts" and continued to be puzzled by those who inquired (at least more politely and less threateningly) as to the abstract matters lying behind the concrete facts. We find once again different "mental sets", different "wave lengths", different aspects of the whole that do not easily come together and do not easily find a common point of mutual comprehension.

Documentation. Another key word along with facts and information is "documentation", which deals with an original or official paper relied upon as proof. When Gandhi went to London to study law, his mother was very worried that the impurities of Western society might have an effect on him. To appease her and before he was allowed to go, he took the three vows, swearing "not to touch wine, women and meat." He went on to explain: "I had been advised to collect certificates of my having abstained from meat, and I asked the English friend to give me one. He gladly gave it and I treasured it for some time. But when I saw later that one could get such a certificate in spite of being a meat-eater, it lost all its charm for me. If my word was not to be trusted, where was the use of possessing a certificate in the matter?"[5]

As with all characteristics and assets, they can be carried to an absurd degree. Gandhi was a highly developed person who came to embody the qualities of several ray types. With highly developed persons it is frequently very difficult to determine the ray of the mind, since they have at their disposal several of the ray energies. Looking at the period when they are especially focussed on the development of the mental faculties, late teens and early twenties, the ray type of mind frequently emerges very clearly. It emerges in mistakes of over-emphasis, as Gandhi's treasuring the certificate, as well as in developing skills and assets.

In the writing of his autobiography Gandhi selected a very factual presentation—a style indicative of the first ray mind. In sharp contrast to this the creative and artistically inclined fourth ray mind tends to be more concerned with the inner life of mood and personal sensitivity on one level, and psychological insight and deep meaning on another level. The *Confessions* of Jean Jacques Rousseau, for example, or the *Letters* of Vincent Van Gogh are filled with an effusive, sensitive account of inner feelings, thoughts, moods, joys, sufferings, loves, etc., telling us much about the inner, psychological state but lacking a clear reporting of outer events and situations. The first ray mind, as we have seen, likes to stick to the facts, letting the facts speak for themselves.

Organizing and Conducting Institutions. When Gandhi was studying law in London, he sought out vegetarian restaurants and soon met other people who were also vegetarians. "Full of the neophyte's zeal for vegetarianism," Gandhi reported, "I decided to start a vegetarian club in my locality . . . I invited Sir Edwin Arnold . . . to be Vice-President, Dr. Oldfield who was Editor of *The Vegetarian,* became President. I myself became the Secretary. The club went well for a while, but it came to an end in the course of a few months. For I left the locality, according to my custom of moving from place to place periodically. But this brief and modest experience gave me some little training in organizing and conducting institutions."[6] This is one of the major contributions of the first ray type and it constitutes a vast field of work. The organizing and conducting of institutions is administrative work. All types are involved in institutions; institutions employ all types. But the work of setting up, administering and maintaining an institution, the work of forming its structure, setting objectives, rules, regulations, procedure, legal relationships, etc. is work of a first ray kind (and also a seventh ray kind) and tends to attract the first ray mind. Fourth and fifth ray minds, however, may also prove to have some skills in these areas particularly when influenced by the first and/or seventh rays at the personality and egoic (soul) level.

When Gandhi was employed in South Africa, he quickly experienced the white man's prejudice against the "colored" in trains, coaches, eating places, hotels, etc. The first thing he did towards the solution of this problem was to get in touch with certain key individuals. Of one person he said that "there was no public movement that could be conducted without him. I made his acquaintance the very first week and told him of my intention to get in touch with every Indian in Pretoria. I expressed a desire to study the conditions of Indians there, and asked for his help in my work, which he gladly agreed to give." Gandhi's next step was to "call a meeting of all the Indians in Pretoria and present to them a picture of their condition in the Transvaal. .... I suggested, in conclusion, the formation of an association to make representations to the authorities concerned in respect of the hardship of the Indian settlers, and offered to place at its disposal as much of my time and service as was possible."[7]

Here we see Gandhi's first ray mind working along certain channels of organization and power. After identifying the problem, he got in touch with key individuals, individuals who were already in prominent (power) positions in the community, in order to get their moral and political support, which would be a key factor in attracting financial support. He then made a study of the problems and got in touch with as many of the people who were affected by the problem as possible. A general meeting was called, the problem once again articulated, and an association, an institution, was formed—a procedure easy for some and so difficult for others. The next step was to set up communication from their new, collective and much more powerful position with the power structure that opposed them or that allowed certain injustices to occur. First he contacted an intermediary, a British agent, who "had sympathy for the Indians, but he had very little influence. However, he agreed to help us as best as he could, and invited me to meet him whenever I wished."[8] Next Gandhi contacted the railway authorities and "told them that, even under their own regulations, the dissabilities about travelling under which the Indians laboured could not be justified." And thus the battle began—unemotional, polite, legal, to the point, and from a collective, institutionalized base of power.

At this point the rays conditioning other "units" or "bodies" of Gandhi's psychological equipment were beginning to manifest in a dynamic way. Precisely what they were is difficult to say from a study of the written word alone. Gandhi was a very idealistic person and proved to be uncompromisingly devoted to the ideal. He could compromise on method, strategy and timing, but not on the ideal itself. He brought a dynamic idealism to whatever he touched, be it business, education, health, politics or government. This is strongly suggestive of the presence of the sixth ray. The concern with the ideal was not the major concern of his life, however, for he considered himself above all a practical idealist, as we shall see. If the ideal could not be made practical, that is, anchored on the physical plane, then he did not spend much of his thought, time and energy upon it. Wherever Gandhi went—England, South Africa, India—he organized others for the purposes of manifesting some ideal pattern of things. His organizational skills, his ability to deal with physical plane problems on a large and significant scale were highly developed. Although he was concerned with vegetarianism, business, education and health fields, his major contribution was in the area of politics and government. It seems probable that the first and seventh rays were prominent in his life. Speculatively, then, we might have an example here of a first ray soul, seventh ray personality, first ray mind, sixth ray emotional body and either a third or seventh ray physical body.

It is interesting to note that whenever Gandhi organized an institution, he did so in an inclusive way. He was not fighting for the rights of a particular group so much as he was fighting for a justice that affected and included everyone. He emphasized love and cooperation, not hatred and separation. He never succumbed to the polarizing attitude of we-are-all-right and they-are-all-wrong. He tried to look at himself, his own group, from the point of view of the opposing group in order to determine where criticism was justified and where his own group needed refinement. For example, in his initial speech to the group of Indian merchants in South Africa he insisted that a greater effort be made to "observe truthfulness in business" and he "strongly contested the position . . . that pure truth is out of the question in business." He also found "our people's habits to be unsanitary as compared with those of the Englishmen around them and drew attention to it. I laid stress on the necessity of forgetting all distinctions such as Hindus, Musalmaus, Parsis, Christians, Gujaratis, Madrasis, Punjabis, Sindhis, Kachchhis, Surtis and so on."[9] The ability to look analytically, critically and objectively at one's own personality suggests that one is gaining distance from it and control over it via the next higher or more refined level of consciousness, which has been called the soul. The ability to look critically, objectively and inclusively at one's own group (racial, national, religious, etc.) suggests a further development of this higher level of consciousness. Gandhi was *manifesting* a level of consciousness that others were vaguely sensing.

Some Areas of Study and Activity. In summation Gandhi wrote: "My stay in Pretoria enabled me to make a deep study of the social, economic and political conditions of the Indian in the Transvaal and the Orange Free State. I had no idea that this study was to be of invaluable service to me in the future."[10] One can have an abstract and philosophical interest (4th ray) in the areas of sociology, economics and politics, a scientific interest (5th ray), or a practical, more immediate and dynamic interest (1st ray). The areas themselves are primarily on the one-three-seven line.

The Year's study in Pretoria was a most valuable experience in my life. Here it was that I had opportunities of learning public work and acquired some measure of my capacity for it. Here it was that the religious spirit within me became a living force, and here too I acquired a true knowledge of legal practice. Here I learnt the things that a junior barrister learns in a senior barrister's chamber, and here I also gained confidence that I should not after all fail as a lawyer. It was likewise here that I learnt the secret of success as a lawyer.[11]

Generally speaking, "public work" attracts the first ray type far more than the fourth or fifth ray types. It is interesting also that Gandhi's summation—"the religious *spirit* within me became a *living force*" (my italics)—characterizes the religious experience in first ray terms. The fourth ray mind would tend to see it—unlike Gandhi's living, vital, practical, dynamic force—more in terms of a mystic union, an inner, transcendental experience, a profound insight. And here Gandhi gained experience as a lawyer. Law, which is essential to governing, attracts many first ray minds.

After two men were acquitted because it was "difficult in South Africa to get a white jury to convict a white offender against coloured men," Gandhi became quite upset. "I got disgusted with the legal profession. The very intellect became an abomination to me inasmuch as it could be prostituted for screening crime."[12] The governing energy of the first ray can be distorted and grossly misapplied by the human personality and intellect. As it is pointed out in Esoteric Psychology:

> Those on this ray have strong will power, for either good or evil, for the former when the will is directed by wisdom and made selfless by love. The first ray man will always "come to the front" in his own line. He may be the burglar or the judge who condemns him, but in either case he will be at the head of his profession. He is the born leader in any and every public career, one to trust and lean on, one to defend the weak and put down oppression, fearless of consequences and utterly indifferent to comment. On the other hand, an unmodified first ray can produce a man of unrelenting cruelty and hardness of nature.[13]

The "first ray man" could refer to the first ray conditioning either the personality or soul. Something of these characteristics and tendencies are also present with the first ray mind.

86

Suppression and Control of the Emotions. Gandhi stated that he was able to attain "great capacity, I believe, for suppressing and curbing my senses, but I have not become incapable of sin, i. e., of being acted upon by my senses."[14] The question of right emotional development and control is a complex and most important question, and one on which esoteric psychology sheds a great deal of light. When Gandhi used the phrase "curbing my senses," strictly speaking and obviously, he did not mean curbing his sense of smell, sight, taste, etc. He meant his "appetites," that is, his desires for some of the things his senses revealed to him. We are dealing here with the emotional-desire nature. There is a tendency for the different ray types to handle emotional development and difficulties in different ways. One way of dealing with the emotional factor is to control it by suppression and inhibition. There is a tendency for the first ray type—the type that does not like the powerless position of being emotionally out of control—to suppress the emotional nature or to approach it with extreme caution. Consider the following example of a first ray mind who got himself into a state of imbalance through inappropriate suppression:

> The client was a man of thirty-four, a dedicated and ambitious lawyer, who had many relationships with women but who until a few months before coming to see me, had never been in love. In former affairs, he had always enjoyed a strong sense of "control" derived from the knowledge that the women were far more deeply involved than he was. At times he wondered if his inability to fall in love indicated some deficiency, but he tended to push such thoughts aside. He told himself that what he primarily wanted from women was "physical sex" and that passion was to be reserved for his work. He described himself, in his dealings with women, as honest and considerate; he was never intentionally cruel . . .

Further difficulty occurred when he met a woman whom he felt he loved:

> Whereas before he had always been reluctant to speak of his feelings, beyond stating that he loved her, he now felt compelled to communicate the depth of her meaning to him. He was appalled at the difficulty he encountered; his mind seemed frozen, the words would not come. What shocked him far more, however, was that

when he did at least begin to speak of his feelings, he found himself struggling not to break down in tears. This happened again and again, to his intense embarrassment and humiliation.[15]

In this case the ability to control the emotions and to function along a mental-physical alignment, by-passing the feeling nature as it were, was carried to an extreme and an imbalance developed. This is something that a great many first ray minds need to take into account.

Gandhi, on the other hand, was a highly developed and "fully rounded" individual and, therefore, is not really a good example of the emotional suppression and inhibition that presents a problem to many first ray minds. Another way of dealing with *negative* emotions, such as carnal appetites, anger, hatred, etc., is to transmute them through the technique of substitution. "The spirit in me pulls one way," Gandhi wrote, "and the flesh in me pulls in the opposite direction. There is freedom from the action of these two forces, but that freedom is attainable only by slow and painful stages. I can attain freedom not by a mechanical refusal to act, but only by intelligent action in a detached manner."[16] Or, in other words, substitution. Gandhi was highly developed both intellectually and emotionally (and also as an integrated personality and a manifesting soul). His developed, positive emotion-feeling nature enabled him to be sensitive to the needs of others, to express compassion, understanding and love—unlike the lawyer described above who wanted to control others and use others for his own pleasure and purposes.

The first ray mind and also the fifth ray mind many times have to deal with problems of a lack of feeling and a lack of sensitivity, whereas the fourth ray mind has to deal with problems of excessive feeling and hyper-sensitivity. On the other hand, there is a tendency for the first and fifth ray minds to achieve more readily a mental focus and to refine the reasoning powers (particularly the fifth ray mind), whereas the fourth ray type, generally speaking, achieves this with greater difficulty. One of the major reasons for this is to be found in the relationship between the planes and the rays.[17]

When adolescent youths are going through stages of emotional development, literature can have an important, edifying influence on all the ray types. Generally speaking, however, it is the fourth ray mind that is especially attracted to the fields of creative writing and to the appreciation of language as an art form. In the field of education literature, as a means of bringing about what used to be called moral development and is now referred to more frequently in terms of values, can play a very helpful role. On this question Gandhi wrote: "I have never been able to make a fetish of literary training. My experience has proved to my satisfaction that literary training by itself adds not an inch to one's moral height and that character-building is independent of literary training."[18] In the context in which this was written Gandhi was concerned with a non-violent campaign of resistance to British rule (a first ray question). He wanted British run schools boycotted. Indian students eagerly responded, but soon after the initial enthusiasm wore off the lack of education created an inactive restlessness. Some argued that the education in and of itself was a good thing and therefore, in spite of the fact that the schools were British run, the students should return to class. From the political point of view Gandhi was adamantly in favor of continuing the boycott and, as expressed in the above quote, he also questioned the value of the education itself. When speaking of the political issues, his reasoning was perfectly sound and penetrating. "Non-cooperation may have come in advance of its time," he said. India and the world must then wait, but there is no choice for India save between violence and non-cooperation."[19] But when interjecting a comment about education itself—and particularly that aspect of education that deals with the arts, with moral and right emotional development (an aspect that comes more clearly under the domain of the fourth ray)—his reasoning was not so sound. "I have never been able to make a fetish of literary training." The use of the word "fetish" intentionally colors the issue in a negative, prejudicial way. Would it be of any value for an opponent to say: I have never been able to make a fetish of non-cooperation? Although "literary training by itself" may not "add an inch to one's moral height," one could inquire, is there anything that *by itself* adds moral height? Politics and law or the sciences *by themselves* certainly do not add moral height. It is interesting to note those areas where prejudice subtly colors the reasoning faculties. Very frequently they will give one clues as to ray deficiency.

Law, Order and Government.. In clarifying his position on non-violence Gandhi wrote:

> I am not a visionary. I claim to be a practical idealist. Non-violence is the law of our species as violence is the law of the brute. The spirit lies dormant in the brute, and he knows no law but that of physical might. The dignity of man requires obedience to the higher law—to the strength of the spirit....
> Non-violence in its dynamic condition means conscious suffering. It does not mean meek submission to the will of the evil-doer, but it means the pitting of one's whole soul against the will of the tyrant. Working under this law of our being, it is possible for a single individual to defy the whole might of an unjust empire to save his honour, his religion, his soul, and lay the foundation for the empire's fall or its regeneration.[20]

Gandhi stated that he was "not a visionary" but "a practical idealist." Non-violence is not an abstract, visionary goal; it is "the law of our species." The highly developed Gandhi, however, did embody to a degree both of these approaches—the visionary and the activist or, in his words, the "practical idealist"—which again suggests a possible combination of rays one and six. He was, however, primarily focussed in the development and refinement of the practical aspect. In this regard it is interesting to note that Thoreau and Tolstoi (two writers with fourth ray minds) had a significant influence on Gandhi when he was clarifying his non-violent, non-cooperative political philosophy. The developed fourth ray mind is the mind that tends to intuit the meaningful new directions, exemplified also in the case of Rousseau. Gandhi put the ideals into practical action, which required a great deal of organizational skill and administrative expertise.

To the motto: "That goverment is best which governs least," Thoreau added: "That government is best which governs not at all." But that state of no-government was to Thoreau a high ideal attainable only "when men are prepared for it." In the mean time, "I ask for, not at once no government, but *at once* a better government." And what was his course of action for bringing this about? "Let each man *make known* what kind of government would command his respect, and that will be one step toward obtaining it" (my italics). In other words, speak and write about the ideal, and this is what Thoreau did. He worked primarily at the level of *consciousness*, perceiving the idea, building the ideal, refining the thought, communicating the word. Gandhi, as we have seen, proceeded along an entirely different line of political and practical organization and action, contacting prominent and influential citizens, calling meetings, establishing associations, presenting grievances as a collective body to the authorities, etc. Thoreau questioned: "Must the citizen ever for a moment, or in the least degree, resign his conscience to the legislator? Why has every man a conscience, then? I think that we should be men first, and subjects afterward. It is not desirable to cultivate a respect for the law, so much as for the right. The only obligation which I have a right to assume is to do at any time what I think right."[21] Thoreau, in the sounding of a strong second ray, fourth ray and sixth ray note, was concerned with an abstract, archetypal ideal. He was not much concerned with the practical aspects of its manifestation. Instead of dealing with the "dreary reality" and the "really vital situation spread before our eyes" as Addams and Gandhi did, he chose to ignore and to disregard it as much as he possibly could.

Gandhi's non-cooperative confrontation and his appeal to a higher law came only after years of cooperation with British rule:

> Not only did I offer my services at the time of the Zulu revolt but before that, at the time of the Boer War, and not only did I raise recruits in India during the late war, but I raised an ambulance corps in 1914 in London.... I lost no occasion of serving the Government at all times....
>
> I know now that I was wrong in thinking that I was a citizen of the Empire. But on those four occasions I did honestly believe that, in spite of the many disabilities that my country was labouring under, it was making its way towards freedom, and that on the whole the Government from the popular standpoint was not wholly bad, and that the British administrators were honest though insular and dense. Holding that view, I set about doing what an ordinary Englishman would do in the circumstances. I was not wise or important enough to take independent action. I had no business to judge or scrutinize ministerial decisions with the solemnity of a tribunal.... I therefore felt that I sufficiently discharged my duty as a man and a citizen by offering my humble services to the Empire in the hour of its need whether local or general.... I should be

deeply distressed, if on every conceivable occasion every one of us were to be a law unto oneself and to scrutinize in golden scales every action of our future National Assembly.[22]

Thoreau, who was highly developed and refined in his philosophical thought, was a mere beginner at how to deal with that imposing and "insular" first ray institution, the government. "As for adopting the ways which the state has provided for remedying the evil, I know not of such ways. They take too much time, and a man's life will be gone. I have other affairs to attend to.... It is not my business to be petitioning the Governor or the Legislature any more than it is theirs to petition me; and if they should not hear my petition, what should I do then?"[23] Thoreau did take practical action on an individual level according to the dictates of his conscience. He spoke and wrote of his views; he refused to pay taxes. In that way he had an effect on countless others and, therefore, did help to bring about change. But thinking in terms of power moves to alter the structure step by step required a type of energy that was not his path of least resistance.

The tendency to totally dismiss the validity of the work of ray types that are unlike our own, particularly when one is brought into conflict with other ray types, is something that we shall necessarily make note of again and again. Gandhi dismissed the "fetish" that some people have for the study of literature. Jane Addams felt that "lumbering our minds with literature" prevents right conduct. Thoreau ultimately dismissed government altogether. "I saw that the State was half-witted, that it was as timid as a lone woman with her silver spoons, and that it did not know its friends from its foes, and I lost all my remaining respect for it, and pitied it.... [T]he government does not concern me much, and I shall bestow the fewest possible thoughts on it. If a man is thought-free, fancy-free, imagination-free, that which *is not* never for a long time appearing *to be* to him, unwise rulers or reformers cannot fatally interrupt him."[24] Thoreau's view of reality was diametrically opposed to the view held by Jane Addams. What Addams saw as reality, Thoreau saw as something that appeared to be but essentially was not. It should be pointed out, however, that a great many fourth ray minds do not share Thoreau's viewpoint and are very much involved in the concrete worlds, due in part to other ray influences. Thoreau's genius was not a perfectly balanced or holistic one.

Thoreau concluded his essay on "Civil Disobedience" with the following statement:

> I please myself with imagining a State at last which can afford to be just to all men, and to treat the individual with respect as a neighbor; which even would not think it inconsistent with its own repose if a few were to live aloof from it, not meddling with it, nor embraced by it, who fulfilled all the duties of neighbors and fellow-men. A State which bore this kind of fruit, and suffered it to drop off as fast as it ripened, would prepare the way for a still more perfect and glorious State, which also I have imagined but not yet anywhere seen.[25]

Thoreau pleased himself with imagining an ideal future state. He preferred to remain aloof from the dreary reality of the present state of affairs. The fourth ray type of mind, particularly when augmented by rays two and six, tends to have a vivid and creative imagination that is a most vital factor in the process of tapping the intuition. It seems that Thoreau had much in common with the "anarchist turned Buddhist" of Jane Addams' acquaintance. What one imagines and intuits now and firmly anchors in the collective consciousness will certainly condition future actions.

Carrying Out Orders. Thoreau, as we have seen, preferred to rely solely on his own sense of right and wrong, his own conscience. Gandhi, on the other hand, for a long time did not consider himself "wise or important enough to take independent action", and he felt that he "had no business to judge or scrutinize ministerial decisions with the solemnity of a tribunal." Thoreau's life style was an independent one, aloof from society, and was without direct access to any organized power structure. Gandhi, since he could and would function within a system and carry out orders he might not necessarily personally believe in, was able to have direct access to an ever widening power complex. When Gandhi was a school boy, a teacher prompted Gandhi to "copy the spelling from my neighbor's slate." Gandhi said that he never learned the art of copying, "yet the incident did not in the least diminish my respect for my teacher. I was by nature blind to the faults of elders. Later I came to know of many other failings of this teacher, but my regard for him remained the same. For I had learnt to carry out the orders of elders, not to scan their actions."[26] Generally speaking, the first ray type of mind tends to appreciate the hierarchical chain of command implicit or explicit in any power structure or organized activity better than the other two types.

The "Intensely Direct Action" of the Buddha and the Christ. Gandhi's interpretation of religion was clearly colored by the first ray of will and power. "I do not believe that the spiritual law works on a field of its own. On the contrary, it expresses itself only through the ordinary activities of life. It thus affects the economic, the social and the political fields."[27] Not the world of abstract meaning so much as the world of vital energies is the way in which Gandhi comprehended Diety. Gandhi interpreted the lives of the great avatars not in terms of quiet and secluded wisdom but in terms of political action: "Jesus, in my humble opinion, was a prince among politicians."[28] "Buddha fearlessly carried the war into the enemy's camp and brought down on its knees an arrogant priesthood. Christ drove out the money-changers from the temple of Jerusalem and drew down curses from Heaven upon the hypocrites and the pharisees. Both were for intensely direct action. But even as Buddha and Christ chastised, they showed unmistakable gentleness and love behind every act of theirs."[29] There are clear similarities between Gandhi's interpretation and Jane Addams' interpretation of knowing the doctrine "through the will" and that "revelation, to be retained and made manifest, must be put into terms of action."

Summary. The first ray type of mind, as it turns its attention to things concrete, to governing and to administrating, must necessarily recognize the "paramount importance of facts." In the field of journalism it is important to report significant facts, leaving others to draw their own conclusions. The fourth ray type of mind, on the other hand, generally prefers to discuss the good and bad of it all, what it means, opinion, interpretation, etc. The first ray type tends to be more interested in uncovering the fact and with accuracy of information. The documentation of fact plays an important part in work of a first ray nature. In the late teens and early twenties the ray type of mind frequently emerges with clarity. The first ray type of autobiographical writing is generally characterized by a very factual presentation, a matter-of-fact style. The pronounced fourth ray type in many cases tends to be more concerned with the inner life of mood, sensitivity and psychological insight.

The first ray type of mind tends to tune in more quickly than do the other two types to the work of organizing and conducting institutions. Gandhi came to recognize important factors of power at an early age: Power requires a group effort, existing channels of power must be recognized and dealt with according to certain procedures (Thoreau chose to ignore these factors), prominent power figures must be approached and consulted, the problem must be studied and facts gathered, and new associations must be formed in order to submit grievances and affect change. Other rays present in Gandhi's equipment seem to be the sixth, the seventh and again the first. In South Africa Gandhi studied the social, economic and political conditions of the Indian. It is here that he learned "public work" and gained confidence as a lawyer. First ray energy can be distorted to screen crime or to commit crime. The first ray energy can bring qualities of leadership and fearlessness. On the other hand, it can also produce cruelty and hardness of nature.

There is a tendency for the first ray type—the type that does not like the powerless position of being emotionally out of control—to supress the emotional nature or to approach it with extreme caution. Gandhi did not respond deeply to a literary type of educational training. Gandhi claimed not to be a visionary but a practical idealist. Non-violence he saw not as an abstract ideal but as a "law of our species." Thoreau was more the visionary, intuiting the new idea and clothing it in the appropriately attractive words and presenting it as an ideal to the public. Gandhi's non-cooperative stance came only after years of recognizing and cooperating with the existing power structure. He felt for a long time that it was not his place to "judge or scrutinize ministerial decisions with the solemnity of a tribunal." Thoreau with his fourth ray mind drew vivid and imaginative word pictures but many times of questionable accuracy ("I saw that the State was half-witted, that it was as timid as a lone woman with her silver spoons..."). Unlike Thoreau, Gandhi could function within a system and carry out orders he did not necessarily believe in and as a result he was able to have direct access to an ever widening power complex. Gandhi as a school boy learned to "carry out the orders of elders, not to scan their actions." Generally speaking, the first ray type of mind tends to appreciate the hierarchical chain of command implicit or explicit in any power structure and organized activity better than the other two types.

Not the world of abstract meaning so much as the world of vital energies is the way in which Gandhi comprehended Diety. Gandhi emphasized the political-activist aspect of the lives of the Buddha and the Christ.

REFERENCE NOTES TO CHAPTER V

1. Mahatma Gandhi, *Autobiography* (Washington, D.C.: Public Affairs Press, 1948), p. 167.
2. Henry David Thoreau, "A Plea for John Brown," in *Walden and Other Writings* (New York: Random House, 1937), p. 706.
3. Martin Mayer, *All You Know Is Facts* (New York: Harper and Row, 1958), p. ix.
4. Ibid., p. ix.
5. Gandhi, *Autobiography*, p. 61.
6. Ibid., pp. 79-80.
7. Ibid., pp. 157-8.
8. Ibid., p. 159.
9. Ibid., p. 158.
10. Ibid., p. 160.
11. Ibid., p. 165.
12. Ibid., p. 336.
13. *Esoteric Psychology*, I, p. 201.
14. Mahatma Gandhi, "Non-Violence in Peace and War," in *Selected Writings of Mahatma Gandhi* (Boston: The Beacon Press, 1951), p. 57.
15. Nathaniel Branden, *The Disowned Self* (New York: Bantam Books, Inc., 1973), pp. 15-16.
16. Gandhi, *Selected Writings*, p. 56.
17. For a symbolic diagram of the seven planes see Alice Bailey's *A Treatise on Cosmic Fire* (New York: Lucis Publishing Co., 1925), p. 817. The fourth ray type is related to the sixth plane (the astral plane of emotion and sentience) and to the fourth plane of buddhi or intuition. The fifth ray mind is related to the fifth plane, or mental plane, and also to the seventh, the physical plane. The first ray type is related to the seventh, fifth and later to the third plane. A similar numerical correspondence exists between the rays and the seven sub-planes of each plane.
18. Gandhi, "Reply to Tagore," in *Selected Writings*, p. 112.
19. Ibid., pp. 111-112.
20. Gandhi, "Non-Violence in Peace and War," in *Selected Writings*, pp. 54-55.
21. Thoreau, "Civil Disobedience," in *Walden and Other Writings*, pp. 635-7.
22. Gandhi, *Selected Writings*, p. 55.
23. Thoreau, "Civil Disobedience," in *Walden and Other Writings*, pp. 644-5.
24. Ibid., pp. 650, 656.
25. Ibid., p. 659.
26. Gandhi, *Autobiography*, p. 16.

27. Gandhi, *Selected Writings,* p. 59.
28. Ibid., p. 126.
29. Ibid., p. 116.

Chapter VI
Henry David Thoreau:
Fourth Ray Mind

Henry David Thoreau was born in Concord, Massachusetts, in 1817. After graduating from Harvard in 1837, he returned to Concord and became a close friend of Ralph Waldo Emerson and other "transcendentalists." Transcendentalism emphasized the transcendent or spiritual as the fundamental reality and emphasized that knowledge of the transcendent is gained via the intuition. Intuitional knowledge transcends the reach of the senses.

In 1845 Thoreau built a small cabin on Emerson's land near Walden Pond and lived there for two years. He experimented with a simplified life style, observed the wonders and beauty of nature, and devoted much time to writing. Two books came out of this experiment: *A Week on the Concord and Merrimack River* (1849) and *Walden* (1854). In July 1846 Thoreau protested against slavery in the United States by refusing to pay his poll tax and he went to jail. The next morning an aunt paid the tax in spite of his objection. His ideas on the matter were developed in his essay "Civil Disobedience." Thoreau wrote a journal, a literary notebook, which served as record of his observations of nature and of his philosophical reflections, and which also served as a social commentary of his time. It ran to 14 volumes when published in 1906.

Unable to support himself through his writing, Thoreau worked as a surveyor, as a laborer in his family's pencil factory, and at various other odd jobs. He also worked briefly as a teacher in Concord and as a tutor to the children of Emerson's brother in New York. Long ill with tuberculosis Thoreau died in 1862.

"His Privatest Experience." In the essay "Life Without Principle" Thoreau criticized a lecturer who was too peripheral for

Thoreau's taste. "At a lyceum, not long since, I felt that the lecturer had chosen a theme too foreign to himself, and so failed to interest me as much as he might have done. He described things not in or near to his heart, but toward his extremities and superficies. There was, in this sense, no truly central or centralising thought in the lecture. I would have had him deal with his privatest experience, as the poet does."[1] The fourth ray type of mind has a tendency to "describe things near to his heart," and to "deal with his privatest experience, as the poet does." This is similar to the effusive, confessional style of some fourth ray autobiographical writers, in contrast to the dry matter-of-fact and more detached style of some first and fifth ray types. Thoreau was also asking in a way for interpretation and opinion. Apparently, he was projecting his own type onto the situation, wishing others to be like himself, instead of observing differences of type in a detached way.

"Incessant Business Opposed to Philosophy." "This world is a place of business," wrote Thoreau. "What an infinite bustle! It would be glorious to see mankind at leisure for once. It is nothing but work, work, work. I cannot easily buy a blank-book to write thoughts in; they are commonly ruled for dollars and cents. . . . I think that there is nothing, not even crime, more opposed to poetry, to philosophy, ay, to life itself, than this incessant business."[2] To say, in effect, that business is a crime opposed to life is a strong condemnation, indeed. Rays one, three and seven (will-power, intelligent activity, organization) play a more vital, controlling role in the business world than do rays two, four and six, although all the ray types are to be found in business. The third ray of intelligent activity and adaptability is perhaps the major ray controlling and conditioning the world of business. ("The third ray Masters are working strenuously in the world of business and of finance . . . a new field of spiritual endeavor."[3] The "lower expression" of the third ray deals with "the use and spread of money and gold."[4] D. K. wrote to a disciple: "Your physical body is on the third Ray of Active Intelligence. This was the factor which brought you originally into the business field and has, therefore, inclined you to field work, and organization work."[5]) Of the three types of minds under discussion, the first ray type tends to have the greatest access to the world of business. Thoreau condemned business and also, as we shall see, government and science, which suggests once again a lack of the one-three-five-seven line.

> There is a coarse and boisterous money-making fellow in the out-skirts of our town, who is going to build a bank-wall under the hill along the edge of his meadow. The powers have put it into his head to keep him out of mischief, and he wishes me to spend three weeks digging there with him. The result will be that he will perhaps get some more money to hoard, and leave for his heirs to spend foolishly. If I do this, most will commend me as an industrious and hardworking man; but if I choose to devote myself to certain labors which yield more real profit, though little money, they may be inclined to look on me as an idler. Nevertheless, as I do not need the police of meaningless labor to regulate me, and do not see anything absolutely praiseworthy in this fellow's undertaking any more than in many an enterprise of our own or foreign governments, however amusing it may be to him or them, I prefer to finish my education at a different school.[6]

Jane Addams admired the "conquering business faculty" and those "concrete minds" who "demonstrate the reality of abstract notions." She also equated abstract notions with speculation and propaganda, whereas the businessmen were concerned with the "supremely rational" world of practical affairs. Her first ray mind was a significant factor in enabling her to tune in on the world of business. Thoreau, on the other hand, considered business an "infinite bustle" and a "meaningless labor" that serves at best to keep one out of mischief. The abstractions of poetry and philosophy yield the real profits in life, and the incessant activity of business can be a threat to leisure required for the cultivation of the poetic faculties.

"If a man walk in the woods for love of them half of each day," Thoreau went on, "he is in danger of being regarded as a loafer; but if he spends his whole day as a speculator, shearing off those woods and making the earth bald before her time, he is esteemed an industrious and enterprising citizen. As if a town had no interest in its forests but to cut them down."[7]

If Thoreau condemned the speculating business faculty, he also with the words "idler" and "loafer" felt condemned by them. The term "unsafe rebel" was also a criticism of type noted by Jane Addams. Pirsig noted such criticisms of the romantic or artistic type as "pleasure-seeking", "irrational", "erratic" and "often a parasite who can or will not carry his own weight." And, as Pirsig pointed out, these are battle lines, indeed. It is a disturbing conflict that can be resolved through knowledge of the ray types.

Thoreau was indeed a genius along the particular ray line of two-four-six, with an emphasis on two and four. He could have profited, it seems to me, by an effort to acquire the ray energies that were not readily available in his equipment. "It is of value to students to study the rays *not* represented in the personality equipment. I commend this to your attention..."[8]

Absorption in Study. In contrast to those who like the constant activity of business and/or politics, who feel alive and vivified when people are making demands on their time, Thoreau endeavored to reduce this sort of activity to a minimal. "For more than five years I maintained myself thus solely by the labor of my hands, and I found that, by working about six weeks in a year, I could meet all the expenses of living. The whole of my winters, as well as most of my summers, I had free and clear for study."[9] Whereas the third ray tends to love activity, the second ray tends to love study. One of the vices given for the second ray is "over-absorption in study."[10] One of Thoreau's absorbing studies was that of the Greek poets:

> There are few books which are fit to be remembered in our wisest hours, but the Iliad is brightest in the serenest days, and embodies still all the sunlight that fell on Asia Minor.... It would be worth the while to select our reading, for books are the society we keep; to read only the serenely true; never statistics, nor fiction, nor news, nor reports, nor periodicals, but only great poems, and when they failed, read them again, or perchance write more.... Read the best books first, or you may not have a chance to read them all...
> He who resorts to the easy novel, because he is languid, does no better than if he took a nap.... Books, not which afford us a cowering enjoyment, but in which each thought is of unusual daring; such as an idle man cannot read, and a timid one would not be entertained by, which even makes us dangerous to existing institutions,—such call I good books."[11]

Thoreau suggested that one *never* read "statistics,... nor news, nor reports, nor periodicals"—and it is interesting that these are areas in which the first ray and the one-three-five-seven line in general play a more dominant role. Reading for Thoreau was not an entertainment, a pleasant pastime, "a cowering enjoyment." It was study; there was labor involved. It was a scholarly pursuit, but Thoreau managed to avoid the kind of scholarship that becomes academically dry.

The second ray may bring one into a life of contemplative study. The fourth ray may bring that study into the areas of literature, poetry (beauty of expression) and into creative writing and creative living—as in Thoreau's case. It might also be noted that Thoreau's writings were filled with philosophical and psychological insights. But he chose neither the form of a philosophical treatise nor the scientific exposition of a psychological study. The form he chose was that of the essay and the literary journal.

Critical of Newspapers. The fourth ray type of mind that becomes attracted to the field of literature and creative writing, as Thoreau was, and to a type of writing that is concerned with the "creation of beauty as an expression of truth," may have a tendency to compare other types of writing according to literary standards. Newspapers and journalism, consequently, receive critical abuse from some fourth ray types. Thoreau considered that it was "too much to read one newspaper a week. . . . We may well be ashamed to tell what things we have read or heard in our day. I do not know why news should be so trivial,—considering what one's dreams and expectations are, why the developments should be so paltry. The news we hear, for the most part, is not news to our genius. It is the stalest repetition. . . . Of what consequence, though our planet explode, if there is no character involved in the explosion?"[12]

Journalistic writing is concerned with reporting facts in an impartial and impersonal way—facts that deal with noteworthy and significant events. There are many facts that appear "trivial" but have far-reaching ramifications to those who know how to interpret the facts and read between the lines. A newspaper is not concerned with lofty thoughts, with "one's dreams and expectations", rather there is the concern with day to day developments, which seem "so paltry", so repetitively stale to many fourth ray types. The news, indeed, is "not news to our genius", for such "news" is recorded in other kinds of writing and in other publications. The statement of exaggeration "Of what consequence, though our planet explode, if there is no character involved in the explosion?" clearly indicates a lack of comprehension of the journalistic purpose. The newspaper reporter rushes to uncover the initial facts of, say, an explosion. In following days other facts leading up to the explosion may be reported. Determining the "character involved in the explosion" requires something else, something more elusive, something that is not easily provable, or conclusive, or agreed upon. One gets into areas where contradictory opinions seem equally valid. It is not the function of a newspaper to deal wih the in-depth "character" of an event.

> Hardly a man takes a half-hour's nap after dinner, but when he wakes he holds up his head and asks, "What's the news?" as if the rest of mankind had stood his sentinels.... After a night's sleep the news is as indispensible as the breakfast. "Pray tell anything new that has happened to a man anywhere on this globe,"—and he reads it over his coffee and rolls, that a man has had his eyes gouged out this morning on the Wachito River; never dreaming the while that he lives in the dark unfathomed mammoth cave of this world, and has but the rudiment of an eye himself....
>
> I am sure that I never read any memorable news in a newspaper. If we read of one man robbed, or murdered, or killed by accident, or one house burned, or one vessel wrecked, or one steamboat blown up, or one cow run over on the Western Railroad, or one mad dog killed, or one lot of grasshoppers in the winter,—we never need read of another. One is enough. If you are acquainted with the principle, what do you care for a myriad instances and applications? To a philosopher all *news*, as it is called, is gossip and they who edit and read it are old women over their tea....
>
> What news! how much more important to know what that is which was never old![13]

In the previous passage it wasn't the facts that were important to Thoreau, it was the "characterization." In the above quote it is the "principle" and also that "which was never old." From the first ray point of view that is concerned with such things as the problems of governing, of law and order, of safety and security, such events as murders, robberies and accidents are newsworthy and may have a great deal of significance, particularly to the local community. In spite of the fact that the principle may not be new, the particular event and the particular people involved are new and therefore the community does need to be informed of the event. The community needs to be alerted to the physical plane event of a man having "his eyes gouged out", in spite of the fact that symbolically speaking man may have "but the rudiment of an eye himself." Thoreau was suggesting that seeing is understanding, and the eye—the organ of sight—can be equated with the organ of understanding or of consciousness. They see not; their consciousness is yet dark or dim; their eyes have not yet opened.

There is a very clear distinction between news and gossip that the philosopher should also be aware of. If the newspapers printed gossip, they would have a string of libel suits with which to contend. Gossip deals with trifling or groundless rumor, with distortion of fact. It lacks the intention of achieving clarity of fact. To equate editors with gossiping "old women over their tea" is prejudice due to type and not even good criticism. William Allen White criticized the profession more knowledgeably when he revealed something of the privileges received by editors and reporters through political and business connections in return for favorable press coverage. The facts printed may be accurate as far as they go, but other salient facts may be intentionally omitted. Certainly editors can be criticized for omission of important facts and for distortion through highlighting only some of the facts, but to call them gossiping "old women over their tea" is to *miss entirely the factor of power.*

Ray types do have a tendency to measure and to judge matters according to their own ray or rays, when the matters themselves fall under the jurisdiction, so to speak, of another ray energy. We cannot judge literary writing on a scientific basis; neither can we judge a scientific exposition on beauty of expression. Similarly, a newspaper is not a philosophical essay, nor is it the *Iliad.* And the *Iliad,* "which is never old", is not a newspaper.

Anti-Materialism. One of the contributions of the developed fourth ray type of mind is a tendency to free oneself from the attachments to matter or the form aspect that hinder the unfoldment of man's greater spiritual possibilities. "Most of the luxuries," wrote Thoreau in *Walden,* "and many of the so-called comforts of life, are not only not indispensible, but positive hindrances to the elevation of mankind." The fifth ray type, on the other hand, during some period, struggles with "intense materialism and temporarily the negation of Diety."[14] The lower expression of the first ray type with its "longing for power and authority" and in its "power realized selfishly"[15] can also be intensely materialistic. The note of material simplicity rings throughout *Walden:* "Who knows but if men constructed their dwellings with their own hands and provided food for themselves and families simply and honestly enough, the poetic faculty would be universally developed, as birds universally sing when they are so engaged."[16] It might be admirable to develop the political and scientific faculties universally as well. But, nevertheless, a simplicity of life in harmony with nature is something we surely need to acquire. Rousseau also strongly and eloquently advocated this point.

Tedious Details.   In *Walden* we find the passage: "According to Evelyn, 'the wise Solomon prescribed ordinances for the very distance of trees; and the Roman praetors have decided how often you may go into your neighbor's land to gather the acorns which fall on it without trespass, and what share belongs to that neighbor.' Hippocrates has even left directions how we should cut nails; that is, even with the ends of the fingers, neither shorter nor longer. Undoubtedly the very tedium and ennui which presume to have exhausted the variety and the joys of life are as old as Adam."

Are these details full of "tedium and ennui" which exhaust "the variety and the joys of life"? Governing a municipality includes city planning, which includes a concern for and regulation of the vegetation on municipal property. (The question of beauty, incidently, is vital here and this is an area to which the fourth ray type can make a significant contribution.) It is interesting also to consider how other societies viewed the question as to whether or not natural resources (such as acorn trees) were held individually or in common, privately or collectively, or both.

There is a tendency for many fourth ray mental types to consider the kinds of details that come more clearly into fields more accessible to first and fifth ray types as being full of "tedium and ennui." The details of the form aspect seem to put shackles on the fourth ray's search for character, principles, meaning and intuitions.

Thoreau advised: "Read not the Times. Read the Eternities. Conventionalities are at length as bad as impurities. Even the facts of science may dust the mind by their dryness, unless they are in a sense effaced each morning, or rather rendered fertile by the dews of fresh and living truth. Knowledge does not come to us by details, but in flashes of light from heaven."[17]

Knowledge that comes to us "by details" suggests the reasoning faculties and an emphasis on the lower concrete mind. Knowledge by "flashes of light in heaven" suggests intuitive knowledge. Thoreau's highly developed fourth ray mind, plus his alignment, it seems to me, with his second ray soul, tended to favor the inward-sensing intuitive approach rather than the outward-gathering and observing rational approach of, say, Charles Darwin. Knowledge comes to us both "by details" and in "flashes of light." These approaches certainly do not need to be antithetical; they can be complementary, to the great advancement of knowledge.

On Politics. The fourth ray type of mind in certain cases can have such a strong sense of the ideal in abstraction that it can with difficulty deal with the details of the present state of human imperfection—which in itself can be seen as an imperfection. "What is called politics," wrote Thoreau, "is comparatively something so superficial and inhuman, that practically I have never fairly recognized that it concerns me at all." He had to admit, however, that:

> Those things which now most engage the attention of men, as politics and the daily routine, are, it is true, vital functions of human society, but should be unconsciously performed, like the corresponding functions of the physical body. They are *infra-human*, a kind of vegetation. I sometimes awake to a half-consciousness of them going on about me, as a man may become conscious of some of the processes of digestion in a morbid state, and so have the dyspepsia, as it is called. It is as if a thinker submitted himself to be rasped by the great gizzard of creation. Politics is, as it were, the gizzard of society, full of grit and gravel, and the two political parties are its two opposite halves,— sometimes split into quarters, it may be, which grind on each

other. Not only individuals, but states, have thus a confirmed dyspepsia, which expresses itself, you can imagine by what sort of eloquence. Thus our life is not altogether a forgetting, but also, alas! to a great extent, a remembering, of that which we should never have been conscious of, certainly not in our waking hours.[18]

Admittedly, Thoreau was half-conscious of the politics and daily routine going on about him. He preferred to be unconscious of these matters altogether and only became semiconscious of them when, as an irritant, they grated upon his serene repose. He felt that politics "should be unconsciously performed"—relegated, as it were, to an automatic state as are the biological processes. There are certain responsibilities of government that, once set up and organized, can function almost automatically, but to say that the whole government should be relegated to an unconscious state is preposterous. He might have eliminated government from his own specialized areas of study, but government and governing is a major aspect of the whole and does require consciousness.

The gizzard analogy is a poor one, indeed, and once again reveals a lack of comprehension of the worlds more accessible to the first ray energy. Grit and gravel in the gizzard of a bird perform the function of teeth, which the bird lacks. The pieces of grit grind up the corn and seeds under the pressure of the gizzard muscles and thus *help* the bird to digest its food. Politics as "the gizzard of society, full of grit and gravel," makes little sense. Thoreau reasoned that states "have thus a confirmed dyspepsia"—which does not at all follow. Grit and gravel would tend to prevent dyspepsia, not be a cause of it. Grit and gravel are not negative factors, as Thoreau supposed, they are positive factors. We find here then a certain eloquence, a picturesque and imaginative representation, but also a lack of accuracy. The scientific knowledge was lacking and an appreciation of first ray energy was lacking.

This is certainly not true of all fourth ray minds. A first ray soul or personality, for example, could bring one into the area of politics, and we might then find a balance between the two major lines. The sensitive insight and creativity of the fourth ray mind along with a comprehension of power and of governing could result in an exceptionally able administrator or governor. When the mind and personality or soul are on different lines, however, there may initially be greater difficulty in integrating the energies, but eventually there can be a more inclusive comprehension and expression of all the ray energies than when there is a predominance along one major line.

In Senator William J. Fulbright's book *The Arrogance of Power* there is a more recent example of a conflict and misunderstanding between the first ray and fourth ray types.

> Some time ago I met an American poet, Mr. Ned O'Gorman, who had just returned from a visit to Latin America sponsored by the State Department. He said, and previously had written, that he had been instructed by American Embassy officials in the countries he visited that if he were questioned, by students and intellectuals with whom he was scheduled to meet, on such "difficult" questions as the Dominican Republic and Vietnam, he was to reply that he was "unprepared." Poets, as we all know, are ungovernable people and Mr. O'Gorman proved no exception. At a meeting with some Brazilian students he finally rebelled, with the following result as he described it: ". . . the questions came, swirling, bellowing from the classroom. Outside the traffic and the oily electric heat. But I loved it. I was hell bent for clarity. I knew they wanted straight answers and I gave them. I had been gorged to sickness with embassy prudence. The applause was long and loud. The embassy man was furious. 'You are taking money dishonestly,' he told me. 'If the government pays you to do this tour you must defend it and not damn it.' It did no good when I explained to him that if I didn't do what I was doing, *then* I'd be taking the money dishonestly."[19]

From the limited point of view of the individual type it seems that the conflict between the poet and the embassy official is irreconcilable. With a knowledge of ray types, however, one can appreciate and integrate both points of view. Fulbright's comment that "poets, as we all know, are ungovernable people" is interesting and does suggest that Fulbright was recognizing something of the type-factor. He was also recognizing the conflict that can occur between the first and fourth ray types. Thoreau very outspokenly said: "It is of no consequence whether a man breaks a human law or not" in his essay entitled "A Plea for John Brown." The poet in this case was rejecting the policy of the government to evade "difficult" questions on Vietnam and was relying on his own "policy," his own personal interpretation of events, his own sense of right and wrong. From a power point of view it would be impractical and chaotic if every embassy official or every person who represented the government fashioned his own personal foreign policy on every issue that came up. There must necessarily be some continuity of policy; certain collective stances must be accepted in spite of the fact that one personally disagrees with them. Collective bodies move much more slowly than individuals do, so certain policies can be accepted temporarily while one patiently and skillfully works at changing policy.

On the other hand, where does one draw the line on participation in unpalatable policies? Cannot the policy makers be more alert to the more sensitive and intuitive thinkers among us, and thereby prevent many mistakes and more quickly scrap harmful directions? Fulbright offered the following opinion: "A high degree of loyalty to the President's policy is a requirement of good order within the Department of State, but it escapes me totally why American diplomats should not be proud to have American poets and professors and politicians demonstrate their country's political and intellectual health by expressing themselves with freedom and candor."[20] The poets and professors stand somewhat aloof from the government and are in a somewhat better position to express themselves candidly than are the officials themselves. But what of the officials? Should they sacrifice their personal conscience for the "requirements of good order"? "The State Department," according to Fulbright, "... has many intelligent, courageous, and independent-minded Foreign Service Officers, but I have had occasion to notice that there are also sycophants and conformists, individuals in whose minds the distinction between official policy and personal opinion has disappeared. That, I suppose, is the worst of it: the censorship of ideas after a while no longer needs to be imposed; it is internalized, and the individual who may have begun his career as an idealist, full of hopes and ideas, becomes his own censor, purging himself of 'unsound' ideas before he thinks them, converting himself from dreamer to drone by the time he reaches that stage in his career at which he can expect to be entrusted with some responsibility."[21]

On the negative side the fourth ray type can be the impractical dreamer and the impractical visionary mystic who fails to concretize or manifest his unconventional ideas. We also find him at times recklessly and emotionally independent, unwilling to compromise even on unessential matters. On the positive side we find the fourth ray type as being "ahead of his times" in that he intuits or senses the more meaningful directions, while others are desperately hanging on to outmoded and rapidly crystalling forms. For the first ray on the negative side one may find the "drone", the one who blindly follows orders, the one who allows his own conscience and sense of right and wrong to be replaced by the factor of power, the one who willingly becomes a cog in a machine. On the positive side one finds the first ray type being able to deal intelligently with the problems of establishing a "good order"—not necessarily an ideal order, but within the limitations of the present state of affairs a good order.

Again one can see the tendency of the fourth ray type to focus on the emotional or sentient realm, reaching for the intuition, while the first ray type at the stage of intellection tends to focus on the mental and physical realms. Hence, the inability at times for the two types to comprehend each other's language. Fulbright seems to be an example of a person who embodies both of these energies and is able to reconcile and integrate both approaches within himself.

It is interesting to note that O'Gorman's description of the incident is primarily a description not of physical plane events but emotional plane events, his own feelings and the feelings of others. The questions came "swirling" and "bellowing." His reaction to the *atmosphere* of the traffic outside and the "oily electric heat" was that he "loved it." Being "hell bent for clarity" seems too emotionally charged for "clarity." Being "gorged to sickness" is a bit of an exaggeration if one considers it from a physical point of view, but viewing it as an emotional plane event it is picturesquely descriptive and probably accurate. The embassy man was "furious." If O'Gorman had thought more in first ray terms, he might have pointed out to the embassy man that the government's money comes from the taxpayer. Since the taxpayers were split on the Vietnam issue, he had every right to accept government money as a spokesman for those taxpayers who were opposed to the war in Vietnam.

"What Need to Employ Punishment?" "You who govern public affairs," quoted Thoreau in agreement, "what need have you to employ punishments? Love virtue, and the people will be virtuous."[22] Some fourth ray types have a tendency to emphasize love, patience and understanding as opposed to punishment as a means of preventing crime and correcting law-breakers. Corruption in high places breeds corruption; virtue in high places breeds virtue. But in the *present* state of affairs certainly there is a need to employ punishment. Thoreau taught school for a short time, did some tutoring, never had a child of his own, so his direct responsibility and power in respect to others was minimal. He had a tremendous influence on the generations that succeeded him, and, therefore, from the angle of consciousness we see that he shouldered great responsiblity. But from the angle of dealing with the immediate problems of harmful infractions of law and order he had nothing to do.

The note sounded by Thoreau was predominantly, as mentioned, a second ray and fourth ray note. ("To be a philosopher is not merely to have subtle thoughts, nor even to found a school, but so to love wisdom as to live according to its dictates, a life of simplicity, independence, magnanimity, and trust."[23]) The fourth ray in some other combination would be an entirely different matter. A one-four combination could advocate strict punishment. Also the fourth ray could influence one to swing between extremes of no punishment and too much punishment before finding the point of harmonious balance.

Consider the following passage written by Theodore Roosevelt:

> Yet amiable but fatuous persons, with all these facts before their eyes, pass resolutions demanding universal arbitration for everything, and the disarmament of the free civilized powers and their abandonment of their armed forces; or else they write well-meaning, solemn little books, or pamphlets or editorials, and articles in magazines or newspapers, to show that it is "an illusion" to believe that war ever pays, because it is expensive. This is precisely like arguing that we should disband the police and devote our sole attention to persuading criminals that it is "an illusion" to suppose that burglary, highway robbery and white slavery are profitable. It is almost useless to attempt to argue with these well-intentioned persons, because they suffer under an obsession and are not open to reason. They go wrong at the outset, for they lay all emphasis on peace and none at all on righteousness. They are not all of them physically timid men; but they are usually men of

soft life; and they rarely possess a high sense of honor or a keen patriotism.[24]

It doesn't seem that Theodore Roosevelt and Thoreau would have understood each other very well. According to Roosevelt, there are "amiable but fatuous", "well-meaning", "well-intentioned" persons of "soft life" who "suffer under an obsession and are not open to reason" and who "lay all emphasis on peace." Roosevelt was approaching the concept of type, but he too had the tendency to distort matters by seeing only the negative characteristics of the type he could not understand, the type apparently opposed to him. According to Thoreau, loving virtue and loving wisdom would alter the present state of affairs. "I am convinced, that if all men were to live as simply as I then did, thieving and robbery would be unknown."[25] Virtue and simplicity of life style go hand in hand. Gandhi, it seems was a person who was able to incorporate both of these antithetical views in his life. He was a man of great virtue and simplicity of life style who inspired many people of India to live more virtuous lives. He was not a man of "sort life" but dealt with the political responsibilities of a nation. He did, of course, maintain a police force. According to Roosevelt, it was a question of "righteousness", not peace. By righteousness I believe he meant justice.

> It is true that law and order are not all-sufficient; but they are essential; lawlessness and murderous violence must be quelled before any permanence of reform can be obtained. Yet when they have been quelled, the beneficiaries of the enforcement of law must in their turn be taught that law is upheld as a means to the enforcement of justice, and that we will not tolerate its being turned into an engine of injustice and oppression. The fundamental need in dealing with people, whether laboring men or others is not charity but justice; we must all work in common for the sanest, broadest and deepest brotherhood.[26]

Righteousness and justice include punishment. Those who infringe on the law are punished. Justice, "not charity"—that is, punishment and not love where that punishment is due—is the emphasis chosen by Roosevelt.

One of the differences between these two points of view lies in the fact that Theodore Roosevelt was looking at it from the point of view of the *present* and the *physical plane*. Law and order must be maintained. Those who break the law must be punished. Thoreau was looking at it from the point of view of the *future* and the *realms of consciousness*. *If* certain things would come about (conditionally, in the future), such as policy makers being virtuous and loving virtue, then the state of affairs would be different, because consciousness would be different. Change consciousness and you've changed affairs.

Both are true: To maintain order in the present state of affairs still requires punishment; "law and order are not all-sufficient but they are essential." Looking towards the future, however, there is not only the possibility (the ideal) of having leaders who "love virtue" and who "live simply," there is the *necessity* of having such leaders if humanity is to survive and to evolve. And this will greatly diminish "thieving and robbery." Thoreau, in a sense, was looking to the future, was being somewhat the impractical, visionary mystic. But also in terms of his own life he turned the ideal of loving virtue and living simply into practical realities. Countless others were influenced and inspired by his example through his writing.

Friendship as Indicative of Harmony. Thoreau wrote that even in winter "no weather interfered fatally with my walks ... for I frequently tramped eight or ten miles through the deepest snow to keep an appointment with a beech tree, or a yellow birch, or an old acquaintance among the pines."[27] Rather than an observation or study of a tree, it was an "old acquaintance among the pines." Rather than a detailed analysis of the tree in a scientific sense, it was a feeling for a tree in the poetic sense. Once again there is to be noted the sensitivity not to the form so much as to the sentient or emotional life of an entity, the spirit of an entity. Key words involved in this sensitivity are love or appreciation, beauty and relationship.

> To be alone was something unpleasant... In the midst of a gentle rain while these thoughts prevailed, I was suddenly sensible of such sweet and beneficent society in Nature, in the very pattering of the drops, and in every sound and sight around my house, an infinite and unaccountable friendliness all at once like an atmosphere sustaining me, as made the fancied advantages of human neighborhood insignificant, and I have never thought of them

since. Every little pine needle expanded and swelled with sympathy and befriended me. I was so distinctly made aware of the presence of something kindred to me, even in scenes which we are accustomed to call wild and dreary, and also that the nearest blood to me and humanest was not a person nor a villager, that I thought no place could ever be strange to me again.[28]

This is a poetic description of a mystic mood and of a rapport with nature. It began with the mood of loneliness, the concern over the lack of neighbors near the Walden retreat, and ended with an experience of oneness.

Loneliness is isolation, a lack of relationship. Of the three types under discussion the first ray type is the most prone towards aloneness, isolation and separation. Excessive impersonality and a tendency to manipulate, use or control others can bring about isolation. Also the tendency to be the central, dominant figure can isolate one. The detached intellectualism of the fifth ray mind when carried to an extreme can also result in isolation. The second ray of love-wisdom is the one "which is concerned so fundamentally with relationship."[29] The second ray is also the ray which "basically controls Ray IV "[30] Relationship requires a sensitivity to or an awareness of the life and needs of another person or entity. Where there is no sensitivity, there is no relationship. There are, of course, all sorts of relationships: There are business relationships, causal acquaintances, relationships of expediency, relationships between master and slave or boss and fledgling or superior and inferior, many of which are tinged with fear. Friendly relationships, however, have a special significance, for they contain a sense of *equality, love* and *freedom.* Instead of obligation, ambition, duty, expediency or coercion, one is perfectly *free* to relate or not. Therefore, if the heart (*love*) isn't touched in some way, the relationship will not exist. Where the heart is touched and activated, so to speak, one is more anxious to give and to find meaningful ways of giving than to get. In discerning the need, in meeting the need, one receives the confirmed spark of unity. Regardless of the apparent outer station, friendliness in this sense is among *equals.* The limitation of time and space necessitate an apparent inequality. Recognizing equality is recognizing also something that is removed from the time-space limitation of incarnation.

In overcoming loneliness Thoreau—through his sensitivity, love and sense of beauty—related to nature in perhaps the best way that man can relate and that is as a friend. The friend disperses loneliness. The friendship brings unity, relationship, love and understanding. Thoreau used such phrases as "beneficent society", "an infinite and unaccountable friendliness", "every little pine needle ... befriended me", to describe the mystic mood that transcended normal sense perception and enabled him to relate to nature in a new way. Van Gogh and Thoreau were speaking the same "language" of friendship, of sensitive relationship, of profound feeling for the life manifesting through the forms of nature, rather than precise and exhaustively detailed knowledge of the forms themselves. This certainly was not the "language" of the naturalist, of Charles Darwin for example.

This mystical, transcendent state or atmosphere of profound friendship, of kinship, of oneness, is in a sense a *goal* for the fourth ray type. It is not a goal of the fifth or first ray types, generally speaking, although it does have similarities to the goal of synthesis of the first ray type. This goal is included in the word *harmony*. Thoreau's excursions into nature were marked by this quality of harmonizing with her. Much of his writing had the purpose of communicating this sense of harmony—which included friendship, appreciation of beauty, etc.—thereby kindling the same realizations in others.

Still another way of seeing this quality of harmony and beauty is in terms of "magic and charm": "The echo is, to some extent, an original sound, and therein is the magic and charm of it. It is not merely a repetition of what was worth repeating in the bell, but partly the voice of the wood; the same trivial words and notes sung by a wood-nymph."[31] It was the "magic and charm" of things that arrested his attention and that he found worthy of writing about. The thing about beauty and harmony and magic and charm is that they all defy description and analysis. Harmony refers to a state of wholeness. When the whole is analyzed and defined in terms of its constituent parts, it runs the risk of becoming something else, something less. Although harmony cannot be analyzed without losing something, it can be alluded to or implied. It is seen also in contrast to a state of inharmony or conflict. Unlike the scientist who wants clarity and exact definition, the poet cannot tell us with precision what something is. He can only tell us *what it is like.* As an analogy we can think of a circle with a dot in the center. On the periphery of the circle there are an infinte number of points. At the center of the circle there is but one. All the points on the periphery emanate from the one at the center. The scientist scrutinizes the peripheral points. The poet stands somewhere between the periphery and the central, transcendent point and points towards the center. Every point on the periphery provides not a thing in itself but a way of looking at the center from a slightly different angle. The scientist scrutinizes the echo as a definitive point on the periphery. The poet sees the echo as yet another means of sensing something of the One Life that magically and harmoniously ties all things together. The intellect is the special faculty needed to scrutinize the peripheral points. The intuition is needed to comprehend the point at the center. Both these approaches necessarily overlap and both can be embodied in the same individual.

Racial Harmony. Thoreau took a journey with an American Indian through the Maine woods and wrote about it at some length in his journal. The Indian had learned some songs taught his tribe long ago by the Catholic missionaries and asked Thoreau if he wanted to hear them. "His singing carried me back to the period of the discovery of America, to San Salvador and the Incas, when Europeans first encountered the simple faith of the Indian. There was, indeed, a beautiful simplicity about it; nothing of the dark and savage, only the mild and infantile. The sentiments of humility and reverence chiefly were expressed."[32] The Indian had been characterized as "dark and savage" partly out of fear and ignorance and perhaps partly for political reasons, but Thoreau was endeavoring to say a few words here and there to heal those old wounds and contribute towards an inter-racial harmony. "The same experience always gives birth to the same sort of belief or religion. One revelation has been made to the Indian, another to the white man. I have much to learn of the Indian, nothing of the missionary. I am not sure but all that would tempt me to teach the Indian my religion would be his promise to teach me *his.*"[34] In the effort to harmonize we find once again the sense of equality and the effort to understand those things that are close to the heart.

117

The ability to bring the energy of harmony into human situations is an asset and a service that can be greatly augmented through a *conscious* cooperation with the highest qualities of this energy known to the individual. This book in itself is an effort to harmonize the various ray types in the human family, as well as an effort to bring about a recognition of the ray types. The Tibetan Master D. K. gave the following advice to a disciple with a second ray soul, fourth ray personality and fourth ray mind: "Your mental body is on the fourth ray; hence your power to harmonize and avert conflict, thus acting as a calm centre in the whirlpool of activity with which you are surrounded. This is your dominant contribution to the work; I would have you ponder on this and intensify your effort to play this part and above all to play it dynamically."[35] By "dynamically" I believe he meant not passively, which might be the inclination or path of least resistance, but actively, creatively and with initiative.

"Science with its Retorts." During the excursion into the Maine woods, Thoreau observed one night a "white and slumbering light, like the glowworm's", around the dying camp fire. He realized that the phenomenon, which excited him a great deal, had to be phosphorescent wood. He cut off some pieces and showed them to his companions while they glowed in his hand.

> I was in just the frame of mind to see something wonderful, and this was a phenomenon adequate to my circumstances and expectations, and it put me on the alert to see more like it.... I let science slide, and rejoiced in that light as if it had been a fellow creature. I saw that it was excellent, and was very glad to know that it was so cheap. A scientific *explanation*, as it is called, would have been altogether out of place there. That is for pale daylight. Science with its retorts would have put me to sleep; it was the opportunity to be ignorant that I improved. It suggested to me that there was something to be seen if one had eyes. It made a believer of me more than before. I believed that the woods were not tenantless, but chockfull of honest spirits as good as myself any day,—not an empty chamber, in which chemistry was left to work alone, but an inhabited house,—and for a few moments I enjoyed fellowship with them.[36]

To a degree Thoreau was trying to be scientific in that he was trying to make careful observations: He noted the kind of wood—"a piece of dead moose-wood *(Acer striatum)*"—and gave dimensions of the glow, dissected the wood and noticed that "the light proceeded from that portion of the sap-wood immediately under the back," etc. His observations, however, were not exhaustive and extensive. He did not procure some of the wood for further experimentation. He observed only to the degree to which it came easily and readily and then he "let science slide." And he did this in order to "rejoice in that light as if it had been a fellow creature." The phenomenon had the aura of magic around it and to delve too deeply into the "scientific *explanation* as it is called" would have destroyed some of that magic. For Thoreau had a belief that the woods were "chockfull of honest spirits" and the phosphorescent light fed that belief. He was in "just the frame of mind to see something wonderful", something inexplicable, something beyond intellectual scrutiny.

Both intellectual, scientific scrutiny *and* a sense of the magic, the everchanging, the undefinable, are needed to gain knowledge and solve the mysteries of life. Thoreau was clearly more developed in the latter art. He stated that "science with all its retorts would have put me to sleep; it was the opportunity to be ignorant that I improved." Obviously, however, Thoreau did not actually mean that he chose to be ignorant, for he went on to say that "there was something else to be seen if one had eyes." He said that he chose ignorance but he said it with tongue in cheek and with a twinkle in his eye. He said it to shock, to insert a conflict, in order to startle one loose from conventional thinking and in order to open the mind to new possibilities, new insights. This is a technique, it seems to me, peculiar to the fourth ray type of mind: the fifth ray mind tends towards cautious clarity; the first ray towards diplomacy or established fact. It can be noted also that Thoreau placed himself in the lesser position by saying he chose "the opportunity to be ignorant." The technique of conflict that unsettles the conventional or accepted forms with the hope of awakening new insights leading to harmony frequently places the one using the technique in a lesser or more humble or self-sacrificing position. On the other hand, there may be a smug humility that is not humble at all.

Not Naturalist but Natural Philosopher. The following passage from John Burroughs' essay "Thoreau's Wilderness" further elaborates the distinction between the scientific naturalist and the poetic naturalist or "natural philosopher."

> He says in his journal, and with much truth and force, "Man cannot afford to be a naturalist, to look at Nature directly, but only with the side of his eye. He must look through and beyond her. To look at her is as fatal as to look at the head of Medusa. It turns the man of science to stone." When he was applied to by the secretary of the Association for the Advancement of Science, at Washington, for information as to the particular branch of science he was most interested in, he confesses he was ashamed to answer for fear of exciting ridicule. But he says, "If it had been the secretary of an association of which Plato or Aristotle was the president, I should not have hesitated to describe my studies at once and particularly. The fact is, I am a mystic, a transcendentalist, and a natural philosopher to boot." Indeed, what Thoreau was finally after in nature was something ulterior to poetry, something ulterior to philosophy; it was that vague something which he calls "the higher law," and which eludes all direct statement.[37]

Thoreau in his dramatic and picturesque way stated that looking at nature directly can "turn the man of science to stone." From a physical point of view the statement is, of course, inaccurate. Emotionally and mentally, however, the caricature has some meaning. When the physical form is studied in a rigidly exclusive way, negating the sentient life and consciousness of an entity, then the scientist indeed runs the risk of encasing his life in a stone-like, psychological imprisonment.

Thoreau did accurately typify his own method as that of the "mystic, transcendentalist and natural philosopher" but not naturalist. This does not mean, however, that all philosophers have fourth ray minds, for all types can be found in that field. Also, it does not mean that all fourth ray minds become mystics and philosophers. The type of mind is only one variable among many salient ones.

Natural History—Hasty Schedules and Inventories. Part of the scientific inquiry requires careful observation of the form in the greatest possible detail and classification of the form. Looking at this type of work through the eye of Thoreau's fourth ray mind, we find the following interesting judgement:

> Books of natural history aim commonly to be hasty schedules, or inventories of God's property, by some clerk. They do not in the least teach the divine view of nature, but the popular view, or rather the popular method of studying nature, and make haste to conduct the persevering pupil only into that dilemma where the professors always dwell.—
>
> "To Athens gown'd he goes, and from that school
> Returns unsped, a more instructed fool."
>
> They teach the elements really of ignorance, not of knowledge, for to speak deliberately and in view of the highest truths, it is not easy to distinguish elementary knowledge. There is a chasm between knowledge and ignorance which the arches of science can never span.[38]

Once again, there is something true and there is a distortion due to type in Thoreau's statement. First of all, classification of the form is not a "hasty" endeavor. Patient, persistent and painstaking effort characterizes the developed scientific type. Secondly, classification ("schedules and inventories") is one of the first steps, not the goal, of scientific endeavor. The scientist is not merely taking an inventory of parts; he wants to know how it all works—which is a divine intent. Anatomy, for example, deals with the "inventory" aspect—the categorizing of parts, the separate form, the structure, the position, etc. It forms a necessary *basis* for physiology, which deals with the processes, functions, activities, interrelationships of organisms. One of the results of these long and painstaking endeavors is knowledge that can restore a diseased organism to a whole and healthy state. Another is to see the symbolic value of the intricate form nature that we might come to understand the human psyche and on yet a higher level that we might gain insight into the nature of Diety.

"There is a chasm" wrote Thoreau, "between knowledge and ignorance which the arches of science can never span." I believe it would be more accurate to say that there is a chasm between *wisdom* and ignorance which science can never span *alone*. But science can and does make a great contribution in the work of dispelling ignorance.

One Law, One Form. What need is there to have detailed, scientific knowledge, some might feel, when one can know a transcendent something that includes all the lesser details?

> If we knew all the laws of Nature, we should need only one fact, or the description of one actual phenomena, to infer all the particular results at that point. . . . Our notions of law and harmony are commonly confined to those instances which we detect; but the harmony which results from a far greater number of seemingly conflicting, but really concurring laws, which we have not detected, is still more wonderful. The particular laws are as our points of view, as, to the traveller, a mountain outline varies with every step, and it has an infinite number of profiles, though absolutely but one form.[38]

How does Thoreau *know* that the harmony resulting from the laws we have *not detected* "is still more wonderful"? If we have not detected them can we even say that they are "seemingly conflicting but really concurring"? Thoreau apparently sensed or felt these matters in a mystical way. A profound heart-felt sense of oneness, of perfect harmony, must be of considerable value. Uncombined with scientific analysis, however, it likely remains a vague, mystic sense that lacks practicality and clarity of knowledge. With the scientific mind, however, is not the problem a similar but opposite one? Does the scientific mind lack a sense of the One Life as it becomes preoccupied with the puzzles of the provable detail? The Master D.K. gave the following seed thought to a disciple for meditation who had a fifth ray mind: "The ivory puzzle box contains the many lesser forms, all true to type, conforming to the pattern. They veil a central ball—the seed of life."[39]

Reunification of Art and Science. Consider the following passage from Robert Pirsig's book *Zen and the Art of Motorcycle Maintenance.*

> At present we're snowed under with an irrational expansion of blind data-gathering in the sciences because there's no rational format for any understanding of scientific creativity. At present we are also snowed under with a lot of stylishness in the arts— thin art—because there is very little assimilation or extension into underlying form. We have artists with no scientific knowledge and

scientists with no artistic knowledge and both with no spiritual sense of gravity at all, and the result is not just bad, it is ghastly. The time for the real reunification of art and technology is really long overdue.[40]

Pirsig's phrase "blind data gathering in the sciences" recalls to mind Thoreau's "hasty schedules or inventories of God's property." Pirsig points to the lack of a "spiritual sense of gravity" and Thoreau to a lack of "the divine view of nature." According to Pirsig, there is a need for an "understanding of scientific creativity." In other words, there is a need for understanding the important role that creativity plays in the sciences, which will lead then to a cultivation of this important factor. What science (5th ray) lacks, the arts (4th ray) find more accessible. "Scientific creativity" suggests nothing less than a bridging or blending of these two ray energies in the quest for knowledge, truth and wisdom.

The Poet and "Cosmogonal Themes." In the following passage Thoreau sings the praises of the poet:

> The one who came from farthest to my lodge, through deepest snows and most dismal tempests, was a poet. A farmer, a hunter, a soldier, a reporter, even a philosopher, may be daunted; but nothing can deter a poet, for he is actuated by pure love. Who can predict his comings and goings? His business calls him out at all hours, even when the doctors sleep. We made that small house ring with boisterous mirth and resound with the murmur of much sober talk, making amends then to Walden for the long silences. . .
> We made many a "bran new" theory of life over a thin dish of gruel, which combined the advantages of conviviality with the clear-headedness which philosophy requires.[41]

The phrases "farthest" journey, "deepest snows" and "most dismal tempests" indicate once again the fourth ray tendency toward exaggeration, inaccuracy, yet colorful, picturesque word painting. In the dramatic there is always the element of conflict. "Deepest snows and most dismal tempests" conjure up the dramatic element of struggle and conflict. Thoreau was trying to make a particular point and he did so not with fact but with a creative splash of color and word. Creativity in many cases tends to be the path of least resistance for the fourth ray mind, whereas the gathering of accurate fact tends to be too dull, too tedious, or too difficult. The poet, he wrote, is "actuated by pure love", which enables him to be undaunted by the physical elements. I would think *pure will* would be the greater impetus in this type of endeavor, and therefore the soldier or reporter among those he lists might go farther and have greater endurance. Of course it was the poet that came the farthest through deepest snows to visit Thoreau, since he himself was a poet. "Who can predict his comings and goings?" Of the three types under discussion the fourth ray type tends to be the least predictable. There is a tendency towards impulsiveness among some fourth ray types, doing things on the spur of the moment, in contrast to the more orderly, planned and organized lives of the other types—speaking generally. The conviviality of friendship, the philosophical discussions that explore the meaning of life—these factors are close to the hearts of many fourth ray types.

> Sometimes dragging sixty feet of line about the pond . . . I drifted in the gentle night breeze, now and then feeling a slight vibration along it, indicative of some life prowling about its extremity, of dull uncertain blundering purpose there, and slow to make up its mind. At length you slowly raise, pulling hand over hand, some horned pout squeaking and squirming to the upper air. It was very queer, especially in dark nights, when your thoughts had wandered to vast and cosmogonal themes in other spheres, to feel this faint jerk, which came to interrupt your dreams and link you to Nature again. It seemed as if I might next cast my line upward into the air, as well as downward into this element, which was scarcely more dense. Thus I caught two fishes as it were with one hook.[42]

Casting the line of meditative thought upward into abstract worlds of truth and beauty, he found that the physical world was "scarcely more dense." Whereas Darwin's "power to follow a long and purely abstract train of thought was very limited", and Jane Addams preferred the "really living world" in contrast to "shadowy reflections" of it, Thoreau was quite at home in the world of abstraction. There are, of course, other very important elements here besides the fourth ray mind, some of which we can identify. The third volume of *A Treatise on the Seven Rays* is entitled *Esoteric Astrology*. It is a complementary volume to

124

the first two on esoteric psychology, and it outlines a further refinement of the interplay of the seven rays on various levels. In the effort of the fourth ray mind to align with the fourth or intuitional plane, the sixth ray energy of Neptune plays an important part. Its presence can be detected in the passage quoted above. Neptune deals with the "mystical consciousness or that innate sensitivity which leads unerringly to the higher vision."[43] Neptune also deals with the transmutation of emotional-desire into love-aspiration and brings about a dedication and orientation to the soul consciousness.[44]

Summary. The fourth ray type of mind generally has a stronger preference to talk about one's "privatest experience" than do the other two types. The autobiographical writing style of the fourth ray type may tend to be effusive and confessional rather than dry and matter-of-fact. Among some fourth ray types there may be a lack of understanding of the activity, purpose and energy of business and a tendency to criticize or see only the negative characteristics of businessmen. Thoreau was sensitive to the accusations of being a "loafer" or "idler." Thoreau considered business an "infinite bustle" and a "meaningless labor" that serves at best to keep one out of mischief. He felt that the abstractions of poetry and philosophy yield the real profits in life. Thoreau arranged his life in such a way that the majority of the time was "free and clear for study," which strongly suggests a second ray influence. In regard to reading, Thoreau suggested "never statistics, not fiction, nor news, nor reports, nor periodicals, but only great poems" should be read. In this selection there was a negation of those areas in which the one-three-five-seven line plays a more dominant role and an emphasis on creative writing (fourth ray) at its best or in its most ideal state (sixth ray). The fourth ray type of mind may tend to consider journalist writing as being "trivial" and "paltry." Thoreau preferred what he called the character of an event to the dry facts. The character of an event, however, can easily slip into exaggeration, personal coloring or distortion and inaccuracy—flaws with which the fourth ray type of mind has to contend.

Thoreau considered luxuries to be "hindrances to the elevation of mankind." The developed fourth ray type may have a tendency to be somewhat mystical or transcendental (especially in conjunction with the second and sixth rays) and may have,

125

therefore, less of a tendency towards "intense materialism" than do the other two types. There is a tendency for many fourth ray mental types to consider the details of the form aspect to be full of "tedium and ennui." "Knowledge," according to Thoreau, "does not come to us by details but in flashes of light from heaven." Thoreau felt that politics (first ray) did not concern him at all. He felt that "politics and the daily routine" should be "unconsciously performed" like physiological processes. In the characterization of the political scene we find a certain eloquence, a picturesque and imaginative representation, but also a lack of accuracy and an injection of conflict. Senator Fulbright noted that "poets, as we all know, are ungovernable people", which suggests a tendency to recognize the abstractions of inner principle over the expediency, organization and order of a political body. The fourth ray type of mind may lack an understanding of the slow, step by step political process that deals with immediate problems due to its own tendency to idealize and envision the future. The fourth ray type can be the impractical dreamer and visionary mystic or the intuitive who is ahead of the times. On questions of crime and punishment the fourth ray type generally leans towards psychologically understanding the criminal and dealing mercifully with him ("You who govern public affairs, what need have you to employ punishments? Love virtue, and the people will be virtuous"). In conjunction with the first ray, however, the fourth ray could be a strict and overly stern punisher. The fourth ray could also influence one to swing between the extremes of no punishment and too much or inappropriate punishment.

The fourth ray sensitivity to harmony can express itself in a profound friendship and also as a transcendental oneness with nature. Since beauty and harmony defy description, the poet relies on analogy and metaphor rather than exact definition. As well as interjecting conflict, the fourth ray type may have special skill at bringing a harmonizing energy into human situations. Thoreau was not the scientific naturalist. His observations were not exhaustive and extensive. He observed only to an elementary degree and then he "let science slide." He preferred to contemplate the poetical, transcendental and magical aspects of nature. A technique peculiar to the fourth ray type of mind is one that assumes a lesser, inferior, more humble role for purposes of teaching others. The fourth ray mind may have a tendency to view science in a narrow way, to think of it as something involved with "schedules and inventories," that is, merely with the categorizing and measuring of the form of things. Creativity in many cases tends to be the path of least resistance for the fourth ray mind, whereas the gathering of accurate fact tends to be too dull, too tedious, or too difficult. Of the three types under discussion the fourth ray type tends to be the least predictable. There is tendency towards impulsiveness among some fourth ray types, doing things on the spur of the moment, in contrast to the more orderly, planned and organized lives of the other types, generally speaking. The physical world is "scarcely more dense" than the abstract worlds to the developed fourth ray type.

REFERENCE NOTES TO CHAPTER VI

1. Henry David Thoreau, "Life Without Priciple," first publshed posthumously in the *Atlantic Monthly* in 1863.
2. Ibid.
3. Bailey, *Esoteric Psychology*, II, p. 731.
4. Bailey, *Esoteric Psychology*, I, p. 50.
5. *Discipleship in the New Age*, I, p. 379.
6. "Life Without Principle."
7. Ibid.
8. Bailey, *Discipleship in the New Age.*, I, p. 351.
9. Thoreau, "Economy," in *Walden* (1854).
10. Ibid.
11. Thoreau, *A Week on the Concord and Merrimack Rivers*, published by the author, 1849.
12. "Life Without Principle"
13. Thoreau, "Where I Lived and What I Lived For," in *Walden*.
14. Bailey, *Esoteric Psychology*, II, p. 42.
15. Ibid., p. 39.
16. Thoreau, "Economy," in *Walden*.
17. "Life Without Principle."
18. Ibid.
19. J. William Fulbright, *The Arrogance of Power* (New York: Vantage Books, 1966), pp. 29-30.
20. Ibid., p. 30.
21. Ibid., p. 29.
22. Thoreau, "The Village," in *Walden*.
23. "Economy," in *Walden*.
24. Theodore Roosevelt, *Autobiography* (New York: Charles Scribner, 1920), p. 534.
25. "The Village," in *Walden*.
26. Theodore Roosevelt, p. 491.
27. "Former Inhabitants; and Winter Visitors," in *Walden*.
28. "Solitude," in *Walden*.
29. Bailey, *The Rays and the Initiations* (New York: Lucis Pub. Co., 1960), p. 613.
30. Ibid., p. 604.
31. "Sounds," in *Walden*.
32. Thoreau, *The Maine Woods*, a volume of Ellery Channing and published after Thoreau's death in 1864.
33. Ibid.
34. Ibid.
35. Bailey, *Disc. in the New Age*, I, p. 275.
36. Thoreau, *The Maine Woods*.

37. John Burroughs, "Thoreau's Wilderness," *Thoreau,* ed. W. Harding (Dallas: Southern Methodist University Press), p. 23.
38. Thoreau, *On the Concord and Merrimack.*
40. Pirsig, p. 287.
41. "Former Inhabitants; and Winter Visitors," in *Walden.*
42. "The Ponds," *Walden.*
43. Bailey, *Esoteric Astrology,* p. 308.
44. Ibid., p. 297-8.

Chapter VII
Thomas Henry Huxley: Fifth Ray Mind

Precision of Knowledge and Severe Exactness. Thomas Henry Huxley was born near London in 1825. His initial career choice was medicine, and he won honors as a medical student at Charing Cross Hospital and Medical College. One particular instructor at the College stood out in Huxley's memory:

> No doubt it was very largely my own fault, but the only instruction from which I ever obtained the proper effect of education was that which I received from Mr. Wharton Jones, who was the lecturer on physiology at the Charing Cross School of Medicine. The extent and precision of his knowledge impressed me greatly, and the severe exactness of his method of lecturing was quite to my taste. I do not know that I have ever felt so much respect for anybody as a teacher before or since ... It was he who suggested the publication of my first scientific paper ... and most kindly corrected the literary faults which abounded in it, short as it was; for at that time, and for many years afterward, I detested the trouble of writing, and would take no pains over it.[1]

Young people tend to be attracted to specific qualities of certain mentors, and very often these qualities provide clues as to type. Huxley was attracted to "extent and precision of his knowledge" and "severe exactness of his method of lecturing." The attraction went deeper than simply admiration—Huxley strove to emulate him. "Precision of knowledge" describes the scientific attitude and energy. The young fourth ray type of mind would tend to be attracted more to a profound feeling for things than a precision of knowledge. Van Gogh, we recall, was attracted to Mauve, an older and somewhat established artist, who had a "fine sentiment" that was "worth so much more than definitions" since "poetry is so deep and intangible that one cannot define everything systematically." One can see that these

131

two men, Huxley and Van Gogh, functioned in different worlds, viewing it from the consciousness angle, and that these two worlds seem initially opposed to one another.

"Bald" and "Luxuriant" Writing Styles. It is interesting to note also that Huxley "detested the trouble of writing, and would take no pains over it." Writing generally requires more than jotting down observations and noting certain facts. Huxley eventually did develop great skill as a writer in his efforts to further the cause of science. In order to do this, it seems to me, it was necessary for him to reach beyond the limits of the fifth ray mind. Leonard Huxley described his father's writing style as "showing that truthfulness need not be bald, and that real power lies more in exact accuracy than in luxuriance of diction."[2] Some fifth ray writing can be critized as being "bald" whereas some fourth ray writing can be criticized as being overly "luxuriant." Certainly Thoreau's writing had a "luxuriance" at times that could well have been trimmed. On the other hand, some scientific writing can be "bald" in that nothing grows on it. That is, it tends not to include the life-side but restricts itself to the barest form around which a degree of "exact accuracy" can be assured. Both approaches would have their claim to "truthfulness", for truth is certainly not limited to precise knowledge of the form.

Medical Student, Zoologist, Ethnologist. The scientific paper that Huxley wrote when he was a 19 year old medical student dealt with hitherto undiscovered membrane in the root of the human hair, which subsequently received the name of "Huxley's layer."Thus Huxley demonstrated remarkable powers of scientific observation at an early age.

Upon graduation he secured a position as assistant surgeon on the H.M.S. *Rattlesnake,* a surveying ship. The purpose of the particular voyage he went on was to bring back a full account of the geography, geology and natural history of New Guinea. According to the reputable professor Vircho, Huxley returned from the voyage "a perfected zoologist and a keen-sighted ethnologist."[3] On the voyage he collected a mass of information on biological phenomena of the South Pacific.

In Conflict with First Ray Type. During the voyage on the H.M.S. *Rattlesnake,* he detected an unappreciative and condescending attitude on the part of the naval officers towards the scientists.

> The singular disrespect with which the majority of naval officers regarded everything that lies beyond the sphere of routine, tends to produce a tone of feeling very unfavourable to scientific exertions. How can it be otherwise, in fact, with men who, from the age of thirteen, meet with no influence but that which teaches them the "Queen's regulations and instructions" are the law and the prophets, and something more?
>
> It may be said, without fear of contradiction, that in time of peace the only vessels which are engaged in services involving any real hardship or danger are those employed upon the various surveys; and yet the men of easy routine—harbour heroes—the officers of *regular* men-of-war, as they delight to be called, pretend to think surveying a kind of shirking—in sea-phrase, "sloping." It is to be regretted that the officers of the surveying vessels themselves are too often imbued with the same spirit; and though, for shame's sake, they can but stand up for hydrography, they are too apt to think an alliance with other branches of science as beneath the dignity—the "Service."[4]

It is generally a considerable shock to the idealistic, though self-centered young people of talent to go out into the world and find considerable obstacles to and lack of appreciation for their well-intentioned efforts. In those youthful years of fragile development, there is a tendency to congregate according to type in order to find mutual support. Apparently, Huxley was somewhat shocked to find "a singular disrespect" and "a feeling very unfavourable to scientific exertions" among the naval officers. According to Huxley, the naval officers considered the "Queen's regulations and instructions" as being "the law and the prophets." The Queen's regulations and instructions were rules of order and conduct, of procedure, of chain of command, etc.—matters that come primarily under the first ray of power. We find here then a conflict or a misunderstanding between the first ray and fifth ray types. Many individuals can function with interest and intelligence in both of these different worlds—especially nowadays that science has become firmly anchored in the established institutions, which was not the case in Huxley's time. But there are a great many who cannot. Since the naval officers treated scientific expeditions with a certain disrespect,

Huxley apparently also responded with a similar tone of disrespect towards military endeavors. He referred to the naval officers as "men of easy routine" and "harbour heroes" and implied that they were quite narrow-minded, having "from the age of thirteen . . . no influence but that which teaches them the 'Queen's regulations' . . . " Huxley responded to their criticism by saying that "in time of peace the only vessels which are engaged in . . . any real hardship or danger are those employed upon the various surveys." But here he entirely missed the point. The danger was not a military one. Therefore, to lose an arm, say, in a time of peace on a non-military expedition would be a mark not of valor but of disgrace, regardless of its scientific importance. The naval officers were concerned with furthering their military careers. Engaging in scientific expeditions was not the way to do it. So these two human endeavors along different ray paths crossed each other with some conflict and with some forced cooperation. Had the men been conscious of the different ray energies, there could have been a learning process of considerable expansion and mutual benefit.

Career Choices. Thomas Huxley was twenty-six years old when he wrote the following comment to a friend: "But it is equally clear to me that for a man of my temperament, at any rate, the sole secret of getting through this life with anything like contentment is to have full scope for the development of one's faculties. Science alone seems to me to afford this scope—Law, Divinity, Physic, and Politics being in a state of chaotic vibration between utter humbug and utter scepticism."[5]

Huxley apparently regarded Divinity with "utter scepticism" and politics as "utter humbug." By Physic he meant medicine, and this field he was able to judge from knowledge and experience. The observation of the "chaotic vibration" of the fields other than science was definitely a bias due to type. He did qualify his statement, however, with "for a man of my temperament, at any rate . . . " There is the tendency to assume that an intelligent person can scan the various fields of endeavor and career opportunities and choose "the best one," as if that were some true and objective selection. Actually, we are dealing here with certain propensities and affinities and certain repulsions due largely to ray type.

Broadly and generally speaking, the fifth ray mind during the stage of intellection and during these times of many career opportunities in the various scientific fields, tends not to look for a career in the fields of law, divinity and politics. This may change, however, when the ray of the personality and ray of the soul begin to have a stronger influence. It may be noted, however, that the fifth ray is associated with theology (see *Esoteric Psychology*, II, p. 42). Albert Schweitzer is a good example of a fifth ray mind who initially contributed to the fields of Christian theology before entering into scientific fields. In times past there were, perhaps, many more fifth ray types who chose to serve in theological areas than there are presently. As it becomes clearer to more and more people that science and religion do in fact overlap and at a certain level can readily be united, perhaps more fifth ray types will make contributions in this important area. It might be noted that a group of disciples taught by the Tibetan Master Djwal Kuhl (the letters to whom comprise the major part of the book *Discipleship in the New Age*) was composed of nineteen fourth ray minds, six first ray minds and seven fifth ray minds. (See appendix for a list of these disciples and their rays. The exceptions to the rule among these developed types included three second ray minds and two third ray minds.) The fifth ray was also present in this group as the conditioning ray of the personality in two cases.

Consider the following reasonings and decision as to career choice made by Theodore Roosevelt as he reflected on a similar stage in his life:

> ... I fully intended to make science my life-work. I did not, for the simple reason that at that time Harvard ... utterly ignored the possibilities of the faunal naturalist, the out-door naturalist and observer of nature. They treated biology as purely a science of the laboratory and the microscope, a science whose adherents were to spend their time in the study of minute forms of marine life, or else in section-cutting and the study of the tissues of the higher organisms under the microscope. My taste was specialized in a totally different direction, and I had no more desire or ability to be a microscopist and section-cutter than to be a mathematician. Accordingly I abandoned all thought of becoming a scientist. Doubtless this meant that I really did not have the intense devotion to science which I thought I had; for, if I had possessed such devotion, I would have carved out a career for myself somehow without regard to discouragements.[6]

Roosevelt was more of an adverturist, an explorer, an out-doorsman, a hunter, than a scientist, which suggests the first ray rather than the fifth. It is not uncommon for a young person to choose a field of study for which he does not have the proper ray equipment. This may be due to parental pressure or to the fact that young people are easily glamorized by a profession. In such cases they rarely get very far and are easily turned away at the first couple of obstacles. What Roosevelt criticized—"studying minute forms of marine life . . . under the microscope"—was exactly what Huxley was doing on his voyage to the South Seas. Yet Roosevelt was dealing with the "humbug" and "chaotic vibration" of politics, which Huxley found so repulsive. Both men were wise enough to realize, however, that perhaps the reasons for choosing one field over another lay not so much within the field itself as within themselves.

Reasoning in a Precise and Exact Manner. In his essay "We Are All Scientists" Huxley described in very simple terms the work-ing of the scientific mind. "The method of scientific investiga-tion is nothing but the expression of the necessary mode of working of the human mind. It is simply the mode at which all phenomena are reasoned about, rendered precise and exact. There is no more difference, but there is just the same kind of difference, between the mental operations and methods of a baker or of a butcher weighing out his goods in common scales, and the operations of a chemist in performing a difficult and complex analysis by means of his balance and finely-graduated weights."[7] To say that "scientific investigation is nothing but the expression of the necessary mode of working of the human mind" is to say that scientific investigation is the way people think, which is true of the scientific type but not of others. To show us that this is a natural and necessary way of thinking he selected a couple of everyday occurrences: that of the baker or butcher "weighing out his goods in common scales." The com-mon, everyday situation he selected, however, is a scientific situation, albeit a very simple one. But if one looks more close-ly, one can see that there is little, if any, scientific reasoning in-volved. A child could perform the operation if told to put enough slices of whatever on the scale until the arrow pointed to a particular number, thus performing the operation by imitation and not by reasoning. Also, the butcher's thought processes are more actively at work when he is wondering how much to charge per pound, how much the market will bear, how much he has to gross in order to meet costs, at what price is the competition selling it, etc., which all deals with questions of a first ray and third ray nature primarily, economic questions, that defy scientific exactitude. But the act of weighing something on scales is a scientific one, as are observations as to the condition of the meat through smell, touch and color.

Suppose you go to a fruiterer's shop, wanting an apple—you take up one, and, on biting it, you find it is sour; you look at it, and see that it is hard and green. You take up another one, and that too is hard, green, and sour. The shopman offers you a third; but, before biting it, you examine it, and find that it is hard and green and you immediately say that you will not have it as it must be sour, like those that you have already tried.

Nothing can be more simple than that, you think; but if you will take the trouble to analyze and trace out its logical elements what has been done by the mind, you will be greatly surprised. In the first place, you have performed the operation of induction. You found that, in two experiences, hardness and greeness in apples went together with sourness. It was so in the first case, and it was confirmed by the second.... You found upon that a general law, that all hard and green apples are sour; and that, so far as it goes, is a perfect induction.... You have, in the first place, established a law by induction, and upon that you have founded a deduction, and reasoned out the special conclusions of the particular case.[8]

In his effort to clarify the scientific method and to popularize science, Huxley discussed the elements of scientific reasoning in a most basic way. The intent was "wanting an apple" or wanting a good-tasting apple. Two experiments were undergone during which time certain observations were made, enabling one to establish a "law by induction" upon which certain deductions could be made.

Huxley went on to say, "In scientific inquiry it becomes a duty to expose a supposed law to every possible kind of verification, and to take care, moreover, that this is done intentionally, and not left to mere accident, as in the case with the apples. ... The method of establishing laws in science is exactly the same as that pursued in common life." According to Huxley, the method is the same but it is greatly refined among scientific thinkers.

It would be a most interesting study to take simple, every-day occurrences, such as the buying of food, the planting of a garden, the purchasing of an automobile, the decorating of a room, etc., and see whether or not the different types approach these matters with in fact different methods and different thinking processes. The statement that "the method of es-tablishing laws in science is exactly the same as that pursued in common life" suggests that Huxley was not observing human nature and psychological processes very closely and that he was projecting his own psychological processes on others.

Certain situations and certain things that we do can be predominantly of a fifth ray or scientific nature and therefore can best be approached via the scientific method. Such as Hux-ley's examples of the butcher weighing meat and the consumer analyzing fruit. Incidently, however, the situation of the drip-ping faucet given by Pirsig is also a scientific one in that analysis of the form nature along lines of cause and effect was needed in order to solve the problem: "John said he had tried to fix it with a new faucet washer but it hadn't worked. That was all he said. The presumption left was that that was the end of the matter. If you try to fix a faucet and your fixing doesn't work then it's just your lot to live with a dripping faucet. . . . He is not stubborn, not narrow-minded, not lazy, not stupid. There is no easy explanation."[9]

Many minds not of the scientific type have problems with even relatively simple fifth ray situations. Then there are an endless number of situations that fall under other ray types and cannot at all be readily probed by the methods suggested by Huxley. A great many artists, for example, rely on a sensitive spontaneity that may spark inspirations and only analyze after the fact and then not too extensively. A great many politicians cannot take the time to experiment and analyze extensively but must commit themselves in certain directions upon insufficient evidence. Both necessarily employ other types or methods of cognition.

Hypotheses, Reasoning, Intuition. Another most important ele-ment in scientific reasoning is the hypothesis.

A man may say, if he likes, that the moon is made of green cheese: that is an hypothesis. But another man, who has devoted a great deal of time and attention to the subject, and availed himself of the most powerful telescopes and the results of the observations of others, declares that in his opinion it is probably composed of materials very similar to those of which our earth is made; and that is also only an hypothesis. But I need not tell you that there is an enormous difference in the value of the two hypotheses. That one which is based on sound scientific knowledge is sure to have a corresponding value; and that which is a mere hasty random guess is likely to have but little value. Every great step in our progress in discovering causes has been made in exactly the same way as that which I have detailed to you.[10]

The scientific thinker endeavors to "discover the cause," to relate cause and effect. In order to do this it is necessary to come up with reasonable, intelligent guesses as to how cause and effect are related. There is a very interesting distinction here, however, between the intelligent guess and the intuitive insight, both of which generate hypotheses. Pirsig wrote: "The formation of hypotheses is the most mysterious of all the categories of scientific method. Where they come from, no one knows. A person is sitting somewhere, minding his own business, and suddenly—flash!—he understands something he didn't understand before. Until it's tested the hypothesis isn't truth. For the tests aren't its source. Its source is somewhere else."[11] Darwin, on the other hand, made the following statement regarding the formation of hypotheses:

> I have steadily endeavored to keep my mind free, so as to give up any hypothesis, however much beloved (and I cannot resist forming one on every subject), as soon as facts are shown to be opposed to it. Indeed I have no choice but to act in this manner, for with the exception of the Coral Reefs, I cannot remember a single first-formed hypothesis which had not after a time to be given up or greatly modified.[12]

Pirsig and Darwin are talking about two different subjective experiences: One deals with intuitive insight and the other with intellectual reasoning. When the flash of insight occurs there may be an agitation or a calm assurance, but there is a deep sense of knowing. The resulting hypotheses, tests, experiments and proofs are not so much to arrive at truth but to prove the truth which one already knows. Intellectual reasonings and hunches, on the other hand, can readily generate hypotheses, but they are not intuitions. These are the sort to which Darwin referred. They are indeed much more hypothetical.

Arthur Koestler has given this matter much careful thought:

> There is a popular superstition, according to which scientists arrive at their discoveries by reasoning in strictly rational, precise, verbal terms. The evidence indicates that they do nothing of the sort. . . .
>
> On the testimony of these original thinkers who have taken the trouble to record their method of work, *not only verbal thinking but conscious thinking in general plays only a subordinate part in the brief, decisive phase of the creative act itself.* Their virtually unanimous emphasis on spontaneous intuitions and hunches of unconscious origin, which they are at a loss to explain, suggests that the role of strictly rational and verbal processes in scientific discovery has been vastly over-estimated since the age of enlightenment. There are always large chunks of irrationality embedded in the creative process, not only in art (where we are ready to accept it) but in the exact sciences as well.[13]

It ought to be noted that Koestler is not differentiating between mathematicians and scientists in the studies he cited. I believe it would be accurate to say that both reason and intuition play an important part in scientific inquiry. Reason is generally more recognized and cultivated. The mental processes that Huxley described are those of reason. The intuition, on the other hand, is the exception to the rule. It is generally not recognized in the scientific community due to its transcendental overtones. Yet intuition plays a most important part in significant discoveries. The fifth ray mind in its path of least resistance cultivates reasoning, which brings the contribution of clarity of thought, precision, strict accurancy, etc. In order for intuitive insight to occur factors are needed that are more available via the energies of the two-four-six line.

D. K. gave the following advice to a student: "I would point out to you, however, the problem which emerges when you have a straight line of contact between the first ray soul, the fifth ray personality, a fifth ray mind and a seventh ray brain. This leads to intelligent high grade work in your chosen profession but negates the free play of the intuition."[14] Intelligent, high-grade work is not always in harmony with the good of the whole, whereas the intuition is. Many scientific remedies, for example, have temporarily alleviated certain problems but then have caused yet greater problems. They were intelligent solutions but not soul solutions or intuitive solutions.

To the same student D. K. wrote: "The ray of your *mental body* is the fifth, and because it is the same ray as that of your personality, you will have to guard with care against mental crystallization, and the undue influence of the critical mind. This ray gives you ability in the field of knowledge, but it must be balanced by the unfoldment of the intuition; it gives you the power to master your chosen field of knowledge, but that power must be balanced by the simultaneous mastering of the world wherein love and wisdom control."[15] The fifth ray mental body brings a capability of mastering a field of knowledge, which is no small endeavor. One must guard against "mental crystallization" and the "critical mind." One must acquire an ability to unfold the intuition, which would necessarily require a relationship with the second or fourth ray energies. D.K. probably alluded to the power factor of love due to the student's first ray soul.

Milton Rothman in his book *Men and Discovery, the Story of Basic Research,* put it in the following terms:

> Creativity is an ability that is prized very highly. In recent years psychologists have realized that a person might score very highly on an intelligence test, but be unable to produce new ideas and inventive thoughts. There is required something in addition—an ability to look at problems in a new way, to look at old ideas and see how they might be changed, to put old ideas together and get new ideas out of them. The emphasis in scientific discovery is the *new idea.* A creative person is immediately recognized as a person who keeps popping up with new and fresh ideas all the time. His mind is flexible and is not covered with an armor-plating which suppresses strange and unfamiliar ideas.[16]

The "armor-plating which suppresses strange and unfamiliar ideas" is another way of describing the tendency towards "mental crystallization" and the "critical mind." The creative person "who keeps popping up with new and fresh ideas" is very likely the one who balances the ability to master a field of knowledge in the scientific sense—that is to know everything that has been done in that field *in the past*—with the ability to unfold the intuition through the energy of love and wisdom, which enables one to see into the future or to sense new and important directions.

While a scientist is in the midst of a series of experiments, unexpected phenomena occur which open up altogether new lines of research. The scientist is faced with the decision of which new interesting line of research to follow. Or should he disregard all of them and stay with the original plan?

> The ability to make decisions like this intelligently is one of the things that separates the men from the boys, the creative scientists from the routine worker. These are often very difficult decisions, because while you are immersed in a piece of research there are so many puzzles unsolved, so many questions in your mind, so many experiments which might be done if you were three people, that you could flounder about in the sea of indecision.
>
> At a time like this it is often a good idea to take a few days off, let the ideas simmer in your mind, go fishing, go talk to other people—and then make up your mind what to do. Making decisions like this depends on so many mental factors that it is more of an art than a science. It is for this reason that a very successful and creative scientist is very similar to an artist.[17]

Rothman recognized the importance of the "new ideas and inventive thoughts" in scientific work. He distinguished between types of scientists in that some were routine workers and others were creative. The worst types were inflexible with an armor-plating that suppressed new ideas. The best were those who were popping up with new ideas all the time. What then are the elements of creativity? Rothman suggested getting away from the work so that the ideas could simmer in one's mind. In other words, when the intellect has investigated and analyzed the subject matter to an exhaustive degree, then other aspects of consciousness must be brought into play. These are brought into play paradoxically through (1) not thinking about it or not intellectually reasoning about it, (2) "going fishing" or doing something that is relaxing, something removed from the usual routine, something quiet, and something preferably within the rejuvenating energies of nature (Thoreau would likely agree with this), and (3) through talking to other people, which *relates* the problem to new energies and also brings in the factor of group energy. Rothman interestingly noted that this was more of an art than a science.

To summarize, the hypothesis in scientific work is a most important factor. It deals with new directions and carries one into the unknown, into the future. It has been called "the most mysterious of all categories of scientific method." One can arrive at hypotheses through intellectual reasoning or through intuition. Inquiries to "original thinkers" have revealed that "spontaneous intuitions and hunches" play a major role in discovery. It is suggested that the fifth ray mind has a facility in developing the reasoning faculties but high grade intellectual work can negate the intuition. The development of the intuition is more the work of the second and fourth rays. The fifth ray type needs to balance the work of mastering a field of knowledge with "mastering of the world wherein love and wisdom control."

Clarity of Thought. Clarity of thought and speech, simple as it sounds, easy as it seems, is not an attribute of the masses and is not a common characteristic among those who graduate from higher institutions of learning. James Spedding (author of a biography of Francis Bacon) wrote the following in a letter to Huxley, telling Huxley of the profound effect that the writings of Francis Bacon had had on him.

> In my school and college days I had been betrayed by an ambition to excel in themes and declamations into the study, admiration, and imitation of the rhetoricians. In the course of my last long vacation ... I was inspired with a new ambition, namely, to think justly about everything which I thought about at all, and to act accordingly; a conviction for which I cannot cease to feel grateful, and which I distinctly trace to the accident of having in the beginning of that same vacation given two shillings at a second-hand bookstall for a little volume of Dove's classics, containing the *Advancement of Learning* [by Francis Bacon]. And if I could tell you how many superlatives I have since that time degraded into the positive; how many innumerables and infinities I have replaced by counted numbers and estimated quantities; how many assumptions, important to the argument in hand, I have withdrawn

because I found on more consideration that the fact might be explained otherwise; and how many effective epithets I have discarded when I found that I could not fully verify them; you would think it no less than just that I should claim for myself and concede to others the right of being judged by the last edition rather than the first.[18]

Francis Bacon inspired Spedding to "think justly", which suggests with impartiality and detachment. Superlatives, exaggerations for the most part, Spedding down-graded into "the positive." Innumerable became "estimated quantities." Assumptions were more carefully considered and the mind was left open to other possibilities. "Effective epithets" were discarded when they could not be verified. These simple yet difficult attitudes of thought tend to be more consciously recognized and acquired by the scientific, fifth ray mind, and the fifth ray mind tends to influence others along these lines. Spedding himself quite possibly had a first ray mind. He shared his insight with Huxley, for he knew that the clear-thinking Huxley would understand and appreciate this factor that had such an awakening effect on him. The limitations of clarity occur when one's clear and certain thoughts become fixed and inflexible or when clarity is accompanied by pride and ambition. In such cases the play of the higher mind and intuition are negated. (See C. W. Leadbeater's *Man Visible and Invisible.*)

Of Sir Francis Bacon Huxley wrote: "Among the many good things to be found in Lord Bacon's works, none is more full of wisdom than the saying that 'truth more easily comes out of error than out of confusion.' Clear and consecutive wrong-thinking is the next best thing to right-thinking."[19] In other words, an experiment may be full of error, but where there is clarity about the error, then knowledge still ensues. Confusion or lack of clarity, on the other hand, tends to result in a repetition of the same error.

Jean Jacques Rousseau with his fourth ray mind described his own thought processes, which appear to be the antithesis of scientific clarity:

My disposition is extremely ardent, my passions lively and impetuous, yet my ideas are produced slowly, with great embarrassment and after much after-thought. It might be said my heart and understanding do not belong to the same individual. A sentiment takes possession of my soul with the rapidity of lightning, but instead of illuminating, it dazzles and confounds me; I feel all, but see nothing. . . .

This slowness of thought, joined to vivacity of feeling, I am not only sensible of in conversation, but even alone. When I write, my ideas are arranged with the utmost difficulty. They glance on my imagination and ferment till they decompose, heat, and bring on a palpitation; during this state of agitation, I see nothing properly, cannot write a single word, and must wait until it is over. Insensibly the agitation subsides, the chaos acquires form, and each circumstance takes its proper place.[20]

Rousseau apparently struggled long and hard to gain clarity of thought. The flash of illumination dazzled and confounded him. His heart and understanding (reason) did "not belong to the same individual." It seems that any profoundly new insight that occurred to Rousseau first tended to agitate the emotional body for some time before calmness and mental clarity could be achieved. This suggests a fourth plane (buddhic-intuitional) and a sixth plane (astral-emotional) interplay and rapport via a fourth ray mind and also via other aspects of his psychological equipment on the two-four-six line (such as possibly a second ray soul and a sixth ray personality or emotional body). The fifth ray scientific mind tends to be more at home on the fifth plane (manas-mental).

"Caution About Mixing Up Observation With Conclusion."   There is a strong tendency, particularly among first ray types, to note a few facts and then to "jump to conclusions", as we have already noted. As regards knowledge, the fifth ray type tends to be the most thorough. It may not always be particularly illuminating or particularly significant, but it tends to be painstakingly thorough. Huxley wrote:

Admiral Mellersh says, "I saw a huge snake, at least 18 feet long," and I have no doubt he believes he is simply stating a matter of fact. Yet his assertion involves a hypothesis of the truth of which I venture to be exceedingly doubtful. How does he know that he saw a snake? The neighborhood of a creature of this kind within axe-stroke is hardly conducive to calm scientific investigation, and I can answer for it that the discrimination of sea-snakes in their

145

native element from long-bodied fish is not always easy. Further, that "black fin" troubles me; looks, if I may say so, very fishy.

If the caution about mixing up observation with conclusions, which I venture to give yesterday, were better attended to, I think we should hear very little either about antiquated sea-serpents or new "mesmerism."[21]

So the developed fifth ray mind cautions us not to confuse observation with conclusion. Our conclusions may simply be faulty observation. Frequently a great deal more observation and study is needed in order to arrive at accurate and clear conclusions.

Science Not the *Summa* of Life. Huxley made the statement that "if, as our race approaches its maturity, it discovers, as I believe it will, that there is but one kind of knowledge and but one method of acquiring it; then we, who are still children, may justly feel it our highest duty to recognize the advisableness of improving knowledge, and so to aid ourselves and our successors in our course towards the noble goal which lies before mankind."[22] Here Huxley made the same sort of error that he did when he stated that "scientific investigation is nothing but the expression of the necessary mode of working of the human mind." In other words, he projected his method onto all others: "There is but one kind of knowledge and but one method of acquiring it"—and here *he* was mixing up observation with conclusion. Since the scientific method of acquiring knowledge had proven itself so many times over through his own scientific method and through the confirmation of many other intelligent minds, it is easy to see how he arrived at that conclusion. But his observations in the area of psychology were simply not thorough enough. Carl Jung, who also had a fifth ray mind, made the statement that "it should not be forgotten that science is not the *summa* of life, that it is actually only one of the psychological attitudes, only one of the forms of human thought."[23]

Authority, Doubt and Scepticism. Huxley wrote that the golden rule of Descartes is:

[G]ive unqualified assent to no propositions but those the truth of which is so clear and distinct that they cannot be doubted.

The enunciation of this great first commandment of science consecrated Doubt. It removed Doubt from the seat of penance among the grievous sins to which it had long been condemned, and enthroned it in that high place among the primary duties, which is assigned to it by the scientific conscience of these latter days....

When I say that Descartes consecrated doubt, you must remember that it was that sort of doubt which Goethe has called "the active scepticism, whose aim is to conquer itself;" and not that sort which is born of flippancy and ignorance, and whose aim is only to perpetuate itself, as an excuse for idleness and indifference."[24]

Doubt—"the first commandment of science"—in the positive sense is "active scepticism whose aim is to conquer itself," that is, no longer to doubt but to know. Doubt then simply states: of this I am not sure, this is not yet perfectly clear, this I do not know for certain, but I actively engage myself with an open mind in the effort to know beyond any doubt. This attitude brings clarity and prevents jumping to conclusions. Doubt on the negative side, however, becomes "flippancy and ignorance" whose only aim is to "perpetuate itself," and it provides an excuse for "idleness and indifference." So the "first commandment of science" can be grossly misused and can corrupt the true scientific attitude. The established scientist who doubts the new in the name of science may, indeed, be perpetuating his own career to the detriment of science.

The question of authority is related to scepticism. Huxley wrote:

The improver of natural knowledge absolutely refuses to acknowledge authority as such. For him, scepticism is the highest of duties; blind faith the one unpardonable sin.... The most ardent votary of science holds his firmest convictions, not because the men he most venerates hold them; not because their verity is testified by portents and wonders; but because his experience teaches him that whenever he chooses to bring these convictions into contact with their primary source, Nature—whenever he thinks fit to test them by appealing to experiment and to observation—Nature will confirm them. The man of science has learned to believe in justification, not by faith, but by verification.[25]

It seems that the nature of knowledge is such that things testified to by others can be taken at best hypothetically and that we only truly know what we have verified with our own experiment and experience. Huxley implied, however, that if we can verify some conclusions of certain investigators that we can accept others without verification, knowing they could be verified if we had the time to verify them. Huxley was apparently at odds with the religious attitude that acknowledges an unverifiable authority testified to by "portents and wonders." It seems to me that he was referring to the work of the sixth ray, and it seems to me also that many of the misunderstandings between science and religion can be traced to the differences between the fifth and sixth rays. Huxley referred to "Nature" as the final authority. Of that "Nature," however, he only knew *a part*, not the whole. One could substitute the word "Life" or "Energy" or even "Spirit" or "God" for the word "Nature" and his words would read the same.

Doubt and scepticism are actually forms of pre-judgement or prejudice and, therefore, strictly speaking, are unscientific. What is needed is *suspended judgement* or an open mind. Doubt is already tinged with conclusion before sufficient data has been collected. The vices of the fifth ray of lower mind have been given as "harsh criticism, narrowness, arrogance, lack of sympathy and reverence, prejudice."[26] Doubt can distort an observation and affect the outcome of an experiment. Doubt colors one's perception, admitting certain facts and excluding others.

There is an interesting example of this reported in the book *Psychic Discoveries Behind the Iron Curtain*. Mikhailova, a Russian woman, has certain psychokinetic or telekinetic abilities that have been demonstrated and filmed a number of times. When demonstrating her ability to move objects through mental concentration she generally begins with something that is relatively easy to move, such as a compass needle. It has been observed that the "force field" or the "emotions of the observers" also play a part in the demonstrations.

"This has been a very difficult point to get over to some scientists," Edward Naumov said. "They expect human beings to turn on like machines. They don't seem to realize their *own* force fields might be affecting Mrs. Mikhailova. She's a very excitable and nervous personality. Some of these scientists with no understanding of psychology or bio-information are radiating unpleasantness and suspicion which she picks up. We're usually able to demonstrate PK [psychokinesis] any time, but with unpleasant people it may take Mrs. Mikhailova as much as seven hours to be able to turn the compass needle. Their negative influence is not helpful. Surrounded by friendly people, the compass may move within five minutes."[27]

When a *group* of doubtful or negative people are observing such an experiment the *collective* force field can have a powerful effect. Studies have shown that positive and negative attitudes affect plant growth. Perhaps some parents have observed how their own positive and negative attitudes towards their children work out in demonstrable ways. The science of how thought affects oneself and the environment will, predictably, be a most important science of the future.

The search for and the insistence upon clarity is a positive and most important contribution of the fifth ray mind. Doubt, on the other hand, generally tends toward a negative attitude of subtle prejudice or blatant criticism, and as such is unscientific. In reaction to the predominance of emphasis upon blind faith and belief during Huxley's time, however, it seems that doubt provided a much needed balance.

"Love of Knowledge" or "Comfort-Grinding Machine." Perhaps a better "first commandment of science" is more truly *love of knowledge*, a quality which Huxley embodied in his life and work. According to Huxley:

> [T]he history of physical science teaches ... that the practical advantages, attainable through its agency, never have been, and never will be, sufficiently attractive to men inspired by the inborn genius of the interpreter of Nature, to give them courage to undergo the toils and make the sacrifices which that calling requires from its votaries. That which stirs their pulses is the love of knowledge and the joy of the discovery of the causes of things sung by the old poet—the supreme delight of extending the realm of law and order ever farther towards the unattainable goals of the infinitely great and the infinitely small, between which our little race of life is run.[28]

"Practical advantage" then is not the true goal of science. Practical advantage is simply a by-product or secondary effect.

The deep, motivating factor is "love of knowledge and the joy of the discovery of the causes of things." "However," Huxley went on to say, "there are blind leaders of the blind, and not a few of them, who take this view of natural knowledge, and can see nothing in the bountiful mother of humanity but a sort of comfort-grinding machine. According to them, the improvement of natural knowledge always has been, and always must be, synonymous with no more than the improvement of the material resources and the increase of the gratifications of men."[29]

The love of knowledge," "Nature," "the bountiful mother of humanity," are factors that are more difficult to define than "improvement of natural resources" and "comfort-grinding machines," for the former are more abstract and border on the mystical. They are, howver, very real and substantial factors to those who have experienced them, as was the case with Huxley. The third or first ray at the personality level in combination with the fifth ray could bring about a tendency to emphasize the practical application of scientific knowledge to bring about strictly material benefits. A second ray influence could bring about a tendency to emphasize the love of knowledge, increase absorption in study, and could also bring about a teaching capacity. It seems to me that the second ray of love-wisdom was a dominant ray in Huxley's life, though I cannot say for certain at what level, personality or soul.

Rothman, too, made note of the distinction between science that seeks to answer some of the bigger questions and science that is exclusively concerned with physical conveniences. "We seem to have lost sight of our original argument—our idea that basic research is done because of curiosity, because we want to find out how the universe operates, and because we get pleasure from the pattern we find in nature. We seem, instead, to be thinking only of getting results, of manufacturing gadgets, of making profits, of changing the world."[30] Thus, according to Rothman, "basic research is done because of curiosity"—but it is more than curiosity; it is the will to know. The "pattern we find in nature" gives us more than "pleasure," it gives us joy. Using Huxley's phrase then we could say that the "first commandment of science" deals with the desire or the will to know thoroughly and conclusively. The second deals with the love and the joy of knowledge. The third deals with painstaking, untiring, keen observation resulting in precision and clarity. For the fourth one could say that it is necessary to cautiously suspend judgement, keeping an open mind, taking care not to indulge in criticism and prejudice, for it is as unscientific to say that something *is not true* as it is to say that something *is true* before sufficient experiment and experience have been undergone.

"Sit Down Before Fact as a Little Child." In a letter to a clergyman Huxley endeavored to clarify his position regarding certain religious matters that the new science was calling into question:

> Surely it must be plain that an ingenious man could speculate without end on both sides, and find analogies for all his dreams. Nor does it help me to tell me that the aspirations of mankind—that my own highest aspirations even—lead me towards the doctrine of immortality. I doubt the fact, to begin with, but if it be so even, what is this but in grand words asking me to believe a thing because I like it.
>
> Science has taught to me the opposite lesson. She warns me to be careful how I adopt a view which jumps with my preconceptions, and to require stronger evidence for such belief than for one to which I was previously hostile.
>
> My business is to teach my aspirations to conform themselves to fact, not to try and make facts harmonise with aspirations.
>
> Science seems to me to teach in the highest and strongest manner the great truth which is embodied in the Christian conception of entire surrender to the will of God. Sit down before fact as a little child, be prepared to give up every preconceived notion, follow humbly wherever and to whatever abysses nature leads, or you shall learn nothing. I have only begun to learn content and peace of mind since I have resolved at all risks to do this.[31]

From a fourth ray (and sixth ray) point of view, the factor of "liking" an idea is related to the subtle feeling of the heart that transcends reason. There is confusion here because the "liking" of an idea as it emanates from personal emotion is no indicator of truth, colored and distorted as it is by glamour and illusion. On the other hand, intuitive insights are indicators of truth, and both the analytical, scrutinizing intellect and the sentient nature play vital roles in the unfoldment of the intuition. Huxley was belittling the religious-philosophical argument by downgrading it to a mere emotion of you-believe-it-because-you-like-it. It goes much, much deeper than that, although on the surface it may appear to be only that. At the same time Huxley was eloquently raising the scientific attitude of the importance of facts to the loftiest levels—or, more accurately, he was helping the non-scientific clergyman gather some small notion of the great importance of facts as seen from the scientific point of view. There is this tendency among all types at certain levels of development to downgrade and belittle the subtle labor of the other types, while appreciating the labor of one's own type. We can recall that Thomas Carlyle did not sit down before facts of nature as a little child. On the contrary, he "thought it a most ridiculous thing that anyone should care whether a glacier moved a little quicker or a little slower, or moved at all." Also Thoreau stated that "science with its retorts would have put me to sleep...." What brought "content and peace of mind" to Huxley put Thoreau to sleep, and Thoreau's method of inquiry was not that of Huxley's. These apparently antithetical approaches, however, become complimentary and then synthesized.

Scientists, Men of Business and Classical Scholars. We are told that "Ray five is the latest of the rays to come into activity and is only in process of 'coming forth to power.' It is steadily increasing in potency, and the result of its influence will be to guide humanity into increasing knowledge. Its energy beats upon the minds of men at this time and produces that stimulation which lies behind the scientific approach to truth in all departments of human thought."[32] Thomas Huxley, it seems to me, provided a significant focal point for the influx of the fifth ray energy during a time of relatively fragile beginnings and new opportunities. Unlike Darwin who isolated himself from the general public, Huxley was in the forefront of the battle, defending, attacking and educating his way through the various obstacles to the new science.

> From the time that the first suggestion to introduce physical science into ordinary education was timidly whispered, until now, the advocates of scientific education have met with opposition of two kinds. On the one hand, they have been pooh-poohed by the men of business who pride themselves on being the represent-

atives of practicality; while, on the other hand, they have been excommunicated by the classical scholars, in their capacity of Levites in charge of the ark of culture and monopolists of liberal education.

The practical men believed that the idol whom they worship—rule of thumb—has been the source of the past prosperity, and will suffice for the future welfare of the arts and manufactures. They were of the opinion that science is speculative rubbish; that theory and practice have nothing to do with one another; and that the scientific habit of mind is an impediment, rather than an aid, in the conduct of ordinary affairs.[33]

It is of much interest to note that the opposition to scientific education, according to Huxley, came from two directions: from the "men of business" and from the "classical scholars." Apparently theoretical and speculative science with its endless experimentation and costly equipment appeared inefficient to the practically minded businessmen. This view did not last long, however, and predictably so, since the one-three-five-seven line can find with relative ease areas of mutual interest and compatibility.

It has become obvious that the interests of science and of industry are identical; that science cannot make a step forward without, sooner or later, opening up new channels for industry; and, on the other hand, that every advance of industry facilitates those experimental investigations, upon which the growth of science depends. We may hope that, at last, the weary misunderstanding between the practical men who professed to despise science, and the high and dry philosophers who professed to despise practical results, is at an end.[34]

The "classical scholars" who were "in charge of the ark of culture" and who were "monopolists of liberal education," provided the other point of opposition to the new science. We might reasonably assume that the fourth ray type of mind predominated in this field, although all types could be found there. The classical scholars concentrated on language, literature, poetry, the arts, philosophy, mythology, religion and related fields. Huxley wrote:

How often have we been told that the study of physical science is incompetent to confer culture; that it touches none of the higher problems of life; and what is worse, that the continual devotion to scientific studies tends to generate a narrow and bigoted belief in the applicability of scientific methods to the search after truth of all kinds. How frequently one has reason to observe that no reply to a troublesome argument tells so well as calling its author a "mere scientific specialist."[35]

There are arguments likely launched by the fourth ray type of mind. Science does not confer culture, that is, it does not confer the refinement of the aesthetic sense and the appreciation of the arts, literature, language, philosophy, etc., usually associated with culture. Science does not touch the "higher problems of life," that is, the more abstract ones dealt with by philosophy and religion. Also science tends to project its methods on all searches after truth and that science tends towards narrow specialization. Note here that the criticism is not that science is impractical. The criticism is rather that science is not abstract enough and cultural enough.

One can see again and again the tendency to measure all things according to the standard of one's own type, which in a great many cases is analogous to saying that orange is wrong because it is not blue.

Political Problems Dealt With Scientifically. Is the scientific method of reasoning applicable in the political fields? Huxley definitely thought so.

And if the evils which are inseparable from the good of political liberty are to be checked, if the perpetual oscillation of nations between anarchy and despotism is to be replaced by the steady march of self-restraining freedom; it will be because men will gradually bring themselves to deal with political, as they deal with scientific questions; to be as ashamed of undue haste and partisan prejudice in the one case as in the other; and to believe that the machinery of society is at least as delicate as that of a spinning-jenny, and as little likely to be improved by the meddling of those who have not taken the trouble to master the principles of its actions.[36]

According to Huxley, one should proceed in politics as one does in science, without "undue haste and partisan prejudice," that is, cautiously and with objective detachment, and with the

154

mastering of "the principles of its action." The machinery of society, however, is not "at least as delicate as that of a spinning-jenny," it is infinitely more complex than our most sophisticated computers. All the more reason to master the field scientifically, Huxley would say. Scientific studies are undoubtedly of considerable help in the political fields. But a great many administrative and power decisions must out of necessity be made long before thorough scientific studies and impartial, nonpartisan decisions are possible. It is relatively easy to gain a scientific understanding of spinning-jennys and computers—physical machines that have no will of their own. Dealing, however, with not only a far more complex physical organism but also with the emotional and mental organism of man, and then on a collective basis—and dealing with it not as an entity removed from it but as a cell interwoven within it—truly makes scientific mastery impossible. As our understanding of the human and super-human mechanisms grows, however, the contribution of science promises to be an ever greater one.

It may be of interest to note that rays one, six and seven are playing major roles in the area of government and politics at this time.[37] This suggests that as well as the ability to handle skillfully power, administrative and organizational matters, there is also the need to incorporate the right use of the ideal as it touches the emotional plane and the masses of men and women. This is an aspect of political life that Huxley was not able to comprehend. Huxley took issue with Jean-Jacques Rousseau's political philosophy that stated that all men are born free, politically equal, and good; and in the state of nature they remain so. Consequently it is their natural right to be free, equal and good. "Due allowance," wrote Huxley, "must be made for the possible influence of such prejudice as may flow from this opinion upon my futher conviction that, regarded from a purely theoretical and scientific point of view, they are so plainly and demonstrably false that, except for the gravity of their practical consequences they would be ridiculous."[38] According to Huxley, all men are certainly not born free, politically equal and good. Infants are born in a very dependent state and: "In fact, nothing is more remarkable than the wide inequality which children, even of the same family, exhibit, as soon as the mental and moral qualities begin to manifest themselves, which is earlier than most people fancy."[39]

Ridiculous as these ideals seemed from Huxley's scientific point of view with his limited knowledge of psychology, "the gravity of their practical consequences" proved far-reaching indeed. The ideal that all men are born equal, free and good reverberated through the soul of man and contributed to the toppling of an aristocratic form of rule with its gross inequalities based on a hereditary caste system. Indeed, the workings of society are far more complex than a spinning-jenny and most.difficult to master.

Summary. As a young man Huxley was attracted to the "extent and precision" of a lecturer's knowledge and also to the "severe exactness of his method of lecturing." In writing styles "exact accuracy" characterizes the fifth ray method and "luxuriance of diction" characterizes the fourth ray method among developed and pronounced types. Huxley demonstrated remarkable powers of scientific observation at an early age. A misunderstanding developed between Huxley's fifth ray scientific mind and the first ray military type during a scientific expedition. Both tended to belittle the work of the other. At the age of twenty-six Huxley regarded Divinity with "utter scepticism" and politics as "utter humbug." As he sought out a career, he eliminated areas more accessible to other ray types. In contrast to Huxley, Theodore Roosevelt's first ray mind had difficulty with the minutia of scientific observation but could deal with the "utter humbug" of politics.

The scientific method includes experimentation, during which careful observations are made, leading to the establishing of a law and the recognition of general patterns in nature. "In scientific inquiry it becomes a duty to expose a supposed law to every possible kind of verification." The scientific thinker endeavors to discover cause, to relate cause and effect. In order to do this it is necessary to generate hypotheses, which can be either reasonable, intelligent guesses based on past knowledge and experience or flashes of intuitive insight. The fifth ray mind may tend to favor the reasoning method over those methods that lead to the tapping of the intuition. In order for the intuitive insight to occur factors are needed that are more available via the energies of the two-four-six line. The fifth ray can bring about "intelligent high grade work" in one's chosen profession. It can lead to mastering a field of knowledge. The pronounced fifth ray type must guard against "mental crystallisation and the undue influence of the critical mind." It is necessary for the scientific mind to cultivate an openness and flexibility and to guard against "an armor-plating which suppresses strange and unfamiliar ideas."

Clarity of thought is an attribute of the developed fifth ray mind, and it tends to eliminate exaggeration and assumption and tends to foster impartiality and detachment. When clarity of thought is accompanied by pride and ambition, the unfoldment of the intuition is negated. "Clear and consecutive wrong-thinking is the next best thing to right-thinking," since knowledge ensues when there is clarity about the error. The developed scientific mind is cautious about mixing observation with conclusion. There is a tendency among scientific thinkers to express doubt and scepticism. The more truly scientific point of view is "suspension of judgement." Doubt already colors the observations in a negative way and can influence certain experiments. On the extreme side doubt can be a flippant ignorance whose aim is to perpetuate itself or it can be idle indifference. The scientific investigator tends not to acknowledge the authority of any given individual, no matter how exalted, but only the authority of verifiable fact.

What "stirs the pulses" of people of science are love of knowledge and the joy of discovery, practical advantage being secondary to these factors. The developed scientific mind tends to "sit down before fact as a little child," prepared to "give up every preconceived notion." The fifth ray is the latest of the rays to come into activity and is only now in process of "coming forth to power." Huxley noted that advocates of scientific education were met with opposition of two kinds: "men of business who pride themselves on being representatives of practicality," and classical scholars who were "in charge of the ark of culture." It was argued that science does not confer culture, the refinement of the aesthetic sense, does not address the higher more abstract problems of life, and usually results in a narrow specialization. Huxley felt that one should deal with the "machinery of society" as one would with the spinny-jenny. In Carl Jung's words: "It should not be forgotten that science is not the *summa* of life that it is actually only one of the psychological attitudes, only one of the forms of human thought."

REFERENCE NOTES TO CHAPTER VII

1. Thomas Henry Huxley, *Methods and Results* (New York: D. Appleton and Company, 1899), p. 9.
2. Thomas Henry Huxley, *Life and Letters,* ed. Leonard Huxley (New York: D. Appleton and Co., 1900), I, pp. 319-320.
3. Ibid., p. 60.
4. Ibid., p. 53.
5. Ibid., p. 101.
6. Theodore Roosevelt, pp. 24-5.
7. Thomas Henry Huxley, "We are all Scientists," in *The New Treasury of Science,* ed. Sharely, Rupport and Wright (New York: Harper and Row, 1965), p. 12.
8. Ibid., pp. 13-14.
9. Pirsig, *Zen and the Art of Motorcycle Maintenance,* pp. 13-14.
10. T. Huxley, "We are all Scientists," p. 17.
11. Pirsig, p. 106.
12. Darwin, *Autobiography,* pp. 140-1.
13. Arthur Koestler, *The Ghost in the Machine* (Chicago: Henry Regnery Co., 1967; Gateway Edition, 1971), pp. 179-80.
14. Bailey, *Discipleship in the New Age,* I, p. 320.
15. Ibid., p. 315.
16. Milton A. Rothman, *Men and Discovery, the Story of Basic Research* (New York: W. W. Norton & Co., 1964), p. 150.
17. Ibid., pp. 76-7.
18. T. Huxley, *Letters,* I, p. 522.
19. T. Huxley, *Science and Culture and Other Essays* (New York: D. Appleton and Co., 1882), p. 74.
20. Jean-Jacques Rousseau, *Confessions* (New York: Brantano's, 1928), pp. 165-6.
21. T. Huxley, *Letters,* II, p. 368.
22. T. Huxley, *Methods and Results,* p. 41.
23. Carl G. Jung, *Psychological Types,* trans. H. G. Baynes (Princeton: Princeton University Press, 1971, Bollingen Series, 1976), p. 41.
24. T. Huxley, *Methods and Results,* pp. 169-170.
25. Ibid., pp. 40-1.
26. Bailey, *Esoteric Psych.,* I, p. 207.
27. Sheila Ostrander and Lynn Schroeder, *Psychic Discoveries Behind the Iron Curtain* (Englewood Cliffs, N.J.: Prentice-Hall, 1970), see Chapter 6.
28. T. Huxley, *Methods and Results,* p. 53.
29. Ibid., p. 30.
30. Rothman, p. 86.
31. T. Huxley, *Letters,* I, p. 235.
32. Bailey *Esoteric Psych.,* I, p. 350.

33. T. Huxley, *Science and Culture*, pp. 9-10.
34. T. Huxley, *Methods and Results*, pp. 55-6.
35. Huxley, *Science and Culture*, p. 13.
36. Ibid., pp. 29-30.
37. Bailey, *Esoteric Psych.*, I. pp. 172, 178.
38. T. Huxley, *Methods and Results*, p. 305.
39. Ibid., p. 308.

APPENDIX
Exceptions to the Rule

In Table One below is a list of students or disciples of the Tibetan Master Djwal Kuhl and the rays given for their soul, personality, mental, emotional and physical vehicles, as stated in the book *Discipleship in the New Age,* I, by Alice A. Bailey. Table Two is a similar list for volume II of *Discipleship in the New Age.* (Of the original forty-one students represented in volume I, twenty-three continued under the Tibetan's tutelage in volume II.)

Table One (*Disc. New Age,* I)

Disciple	Page No.	Soul Ray	Personality Ray	Mind	Emotion	Physical
B.S.A.	05	3	6	5	6	3
L.D.O.	127	2	4	4	2	7
J.A.C.	136	1	2	-	-	-
F.C.D.	138	2	4	1	2	7
J.W.K.-P.	157	1	2	4	2	7
R.A.J.	173	2	7	4	6	2
I.A.P.	186	1	2	4	1	3
S.S.P.	189	2	5	4	6	3
C.A.C.	203	1	2	4	6	1
I.S.G.-L.	210	2	1	1	6	1
L.F.U.	225	1	3	3	6	6
I.B.S.	235	1	6	4	6	3
L.D.N.-C.	262	-	-	-	-	-
R.V.B.	263	2	4	4	2	3
D.A.O.	278	7	1	-	-	-
W.D.B.	291	2	4	-	-	-
D.L.R.	301	1	5	5	6	7
S.C.P.	321	1	6	2	6	1
P.G.C.	342	2	7	5	6	7
R.S.U.	355	2	3	1	1	7
W.D.S.	375	2	1	2	1	3
D.P.R.	382	1	5	4	2	3
G.S.S.	406	7	6	1	6	3
D.H.B.	416	2	6	1	1	7
P.D.W.	433	2	6	5	6	7
W.O.I.	441	2	5	4	6	7
D.I.J.	454	2	6	4	1	7
L.U.T.	471	2	1	4	6	3
D.E.I.	497	2	1	2	1	3

Disciple	Page No.	Soul Ray	Personality Ray	Mind-Emotion-Physical		
C.D.P.	504	2	6	5	6	6
R.L.U.	531	2	4	5	6	3
K.E.S.	544	2	-	4	6	7
O.L.R.D.	551	1	5	3	6	1
S.R.D.	560	2	6	4	1	3
H.S.D.	571	2	1	1	6	7
L.T.S.-K.	595	3	6	5	1	3
B.S.W.	621	1	7	4	6	7
R.S.W.	637	2	7	4	2	7
E.E.S.	645	7	6	4	6	1
R.R.R.	649	2	1	4	6	1
J.S.P.	662	2	6	4	2	7

Table Two (*Disc. New Age*, II)

Disciple	Page No.	Soul Ray	Personality Ray	Mind-Emotion-Physical		
L.D.O.	443	2	4	4	2	7
F.C.D.	459	2	4	1	2	7
R.A.J.	473	2	7	4	6	2
I.A.P.	492	1	2	4	1	3
I.S.G.-L.	511	2	1	1	6	1
L.F.U.	529	1	3	3	6	6
I.B.S.	544	1	6	4	6	3
R.V.B.	558	2	4	4	2	3
S.C.P.	570	1	6	2	6	1
P.G.C.	574	2	7	5	6	7
J.W.K.-P.	588	1	2	4	2	7
R.S.U.	599	2	3	1	1	7
W.D.S.	619	2	1	2	1	3
E.E.S.	640	7	6	4	6	1
D.P.R.	642	1	5	4	2	3
D.H.B.	656	2	6	1	1	7
D.I.J.	681	2	6	4	1	7
L.U.T.	697	2	1	4	6	3
D.E.I.	703	2	1	2	1	3
H.S.D.	713	2	1	1	6	7
L.T.S.-K.	725	3	6	5	1	3
R.S.W.	734	2	7	4	2	7
D.L.R.	750	1	5	5	6	7

As mentioned in the introductory chapter, the three rays of the mind (1, 4 and 5) are "infallible rule, except in the case of accepted disciples." In the list of students above for whom the mental ray is given, there are 6 first ray minds, 19 fourth ray minds, and 7 fifth ray minds. The exceptions to the rule are 3 second ray minds and 2 third ray minds. In the book *Destiny of Nations* (A. A Bailey, p. 38) the Tibetan stated that the Buddha had a sixth ray mind, "a very rare phenomenon." And in *Rays and Initiation* (pp. 570, 574) he stated that a seventh ray mind was a common occurence at a particular stage of evolutionary development. From this information it would appear that the mind can be on any one of the seven rays, although a sixth ray mind would be very rare, indeed.